Florence

Front cover: Brunelleschi's dome
dominates the city's skyline

Right: Michelangelo's *David*

The Duomo • Brunelleschi's magnificent dome towers above the city; equally impressive is Giotto's graceful campanile *(page 27)*

Palazzo Pitti and Giardino di Boboli • A sumptuous palace and delightful pleasure-garden that once belonged to the Medicis *(page 69)*

Santa Croce • This glorious church is full of artistic treasures *(page 46)*

The Accademia • The gallery's star exhibit is Michelangelo's *David*, perhaps the most famous piece of sculpture in the Western world *(page 60)*

The Uffizi • Home to the world's greatest collection of Italian Renaissance painting *(page 37)*

Ponte Vecchio • The beautiful medieval bridge still retains the small shops of its artisans *(page 68)*

Cappella Brancacci • The site of Masaccio's sublime frescoes *(page 72)*

Santa Maria Novella • The cavernous church was designed by Dominican architects in the mid-13th century *(page 64)*

San Lorenzo • The first Renaissance church and home to the glorious Medici Chapels *(page 54)*

San Marco • The frescoed dormitory of the monastery is the location of some of Fra Angelico's finest works *(page 58)*

CONTENTS

26

76

87

88

98

79

INTRODUCTION

The magnificent view from the hilltop church of San Miniato has changed little since the 16th century. The belvedere here looks out across the bridge-trellised Arno to Florence's *centro storico* (historic centre). It is a sea of terracotta rooftops interrupted only by the cupola of San Lorenzo, the medieval bell-tower of the Palazzo Vecchio and the focal point of the Duomo's massive cupola.

The awesome contribution Florence made to Western civilisation and culture is greatly out of proportion to its then diminutive size. Few nations, let alone cities, can boast of having nurtured such a remarkable heritage of artistic, literary, scientific and political talent in such a short period of time. Florence was, as D.H. Lawrence put it, 'man's perfect universe'. The roll call of artists and writers is an unparalleled record for any city; and one whose uncontested period of greatness spanned less than 300 years.

Guidebooks often compare Renaissance Florence with Athens in the 5th century BC, but while that glory is recalled only by spectacular ruins, Renaissance Florence remains very much intact and in evidence at every turn. Its historic palaces, great churches, exquisite sculptures and countless masterworks of art are not crumbling relics, but a vivid and functional part of everyday life – worked in, lived in, prayed in, prized by present-day Florentines and open to all.

Famous sons

Some of the greatest names in European culture – Dante, Boccaccio, Giotto, Donatello, Botticelli, Michelangelo, Leonardo, Cellini and Machiavelli – lived and worked in Florence.

The rooftops of Florence from the Duomo's cupola

The picturesque Ponte Vecchio spans the River Arno

The elegant Palazzo Vecchio, where the first civic authority sat in the Middle Ages, still houses the offices of the city council. Congregations kneel for mass in churches commissioned by medieval guilds. The jewellery stores lining the Ponte Vecchio are occupied by the descendants of goldsmiths who set up workshops here in the 14th century. Most of the city's narrow, cobbled side streets are the width necessary to permit the passage of horse-drawn carts of centuries ago.

Not surprisingly, since the late 18th century, when Florence and its treasures became an unmissable stop on the 'Grand Tour' undertaken by the British gentry, the city has proved irresistible to tourists. Today, the medieval alleys are lined with ice-cream bars and pizza shops, while postcard vendors and souvenir stalls crowd the piazzas, and milling throngs of visitors from around the world cram the streets and museums. But the bronze-workers and leather artisans, although dying breeds, can still be found here in their workshops.

Florence's detractors describe the city as overcrowded and overpriced, and there is a modicum of truth in such criticisms. But the crowds, and to a certain extent the high prices, can be avoided by visiting in low season. And you'll never escape the overwhelming impact of so much superlative art and architecture, even if you have only a few days to see it. Be selective, pick out a few highlights and absorb them at your leisure. If you try to cover everything, you'll end up exhausted, and remembering little.

Trials and Tribulations

The medieval Florentines were described as pragmatic, hard-working, inventive and sharp-witted. These qualities are evident in today's inhabitants, along with an innate sense of dignity, elegance and a savage pride in their city and its patrimony.

The Florentines' resilience has been illustrated throughout history, but never more clearly than during the disastrous flood of November 1966. Swollen by heavy rains, the Arno burst its banks one night, carrying away everything in its

The Medici Arms

Students of heraldry will be busy in Florence, for the coats of arms of wealthy families, trade guilds and sponsors embellish the facades of many palaces, towers and churches.

The most famous, of course, are the ubiquitous arms of the Medici family, with their six balls. The balls are said to represent pills, for the Medici, whose name means 'doctors', were originally members of the guild of spice merchants and apothecaries; they later made their fame and fortune in textiles and banking. Five balls are coloured red, but the top ball is blue and bears the golden lily of France – a gift from Louis XI of France in the 15th century.

Evidence of the city's artistic heritage is abundant

wake. In certain parts of the city the water reached depths of 7m (23ft) – small plaques around town indicate the height of the flood. Thick mud, mixed with damaging oil from ruptured tanks, swirled into shops, museums and homes.

Hundreds of paintings, frescoes and sculptures, and more than a million priceless antique books, were severely damaged, many beyond repair. Before the flood waters had receded, the people of Florence joined in the Herculean task of rescuing what they could. In the aftermath, they helped with the work of clearing debris and repairing the urban fabric; the job of restoring damaged paintings and sculptures was in the hands of an international team of experts (some of them still working to this day). Most works are now back on display in museums and galleries.

The people's resolve was tested once again in May 1993, when a Mafia car bomb tore apart the west wing of the Uffizi Gallery, killing the custodian and her family of four. Thanks to protective plexiglass shields, irreparable damage was limited. Two hundred works were damaged, 37 of them seriously, and remarkably only two beyond repair. The Uffizi's 150-member staff worked around the clock without extra pay, putting the building back in order as soon as possible. As a result, a portion of the gallery was reopened to the public less than two months later. The Uffizi has recently been the subject of a multimillion-euro project that will double the size of the exhibition space and give visitors the chance to see many previously undisplayed works.

It is this sense of being custodians of the legacy of the Renaissance, and heirs to an unmatched tradition of excellence, that gives the Florentines an almost Medici-like pride in their city. This feeling of continuity with the past is what makes Florence such a uniquely evocative place. Its unparalleled masterworks are not viewed simply as isolated museum pieces, but in the context of the city that produced them. They are a living record of an extraordinary period of creativity and innovation.

For this alone, Florence deserves all the superlatives that are shamelessly showered upon it. What's more, if the heat, crowds and queues become too much, you can always escape to a hilltop across the river, and savour the same view that Michelangelo must have savoured five centuries ago.

Florence remains a vibrant, living city

A BRIEF HISTORY

No one quite knows how the Roman town of Florentia came by its name. According to some, it was named after Florinus, a Roman general, who in 63BC encamped on the city's future site to besiege the nearby hill town of Fiesole, which was ruled by the Etruscans, Italy's pre-Roman lords. Others maintain that the name refers to the abundance of flowers in the region, or perhaps even to the 'flourishing' of the successful riverside town.

Whatever the origin of its name, Roman Florence had developed into a thriving military and commercial settlement by around 59BC. If you take a walk along the aptly named Via Romana on the south bank of the Arno and cross the Ponte Vecchio towards the city centre, you'll be following in the steps of the Roman legions, travellers and merchants of 2,000 years ago. And even though you'll find no visible Roman remains in Florence itself (although neighbouring Fiesole boasts a number of Etruscan and Roman ruins dating to the 1st century BC), all the trappings of civilised Roman life were once located here, including a forum, baths, temples and a theatre.

The Romans established the settlement in 59BC

From the Carolingians to the Republic

However, a few centuries later, invasions from the north and the fall of the Western Roman Empire (AD476) plunged Europe into a turbulent period of history. This was briefly relieved during the sway of the Frankish king, Charlemagne, and his vast European empire of the 8th and 9th centuries. By the 10th century, however, even greater chaos had set in.

Somehow the Carolingian province of Tuscany survived. In the late 11th century, Florence made rapid commercial and political progress under a remarkable ruler, Mathilda, the Grand Countess of Tuscany. The great guilds *(arti maggiori)* – influential bodies set up to protect the interests of the apothecaries and the wool, silk and spice merchants (among others) that might be seen as the precursors of today's trade unions – came into being. By 1138, just 23 years after Mathilda's death, Florence had developed into a self-governing republic and a power to be reckoned with.

The well-preserved Roman theatre at Fiesole

At that time, Florence presented an appearance very different from that of today's city. The wealthy merchant families fortified their homes with square stone towers, often more than 70m (230ft) high, to serve as impregnable refuges during the recurring feuds that split the community.

By the end of the 12th century, the city's skyline bristled with over 150 towers. Only a few have survived, but a better idea of the town's early appearance can be grasped in the Tuscan hill town of San Gimignano *(see page 82)*.

Guelphs and Ghibellines

Sooner or later the interests of an aristocratic elite and a rising merchant class were bound to clash, and when they did, Florence's development declined into a series of savage factional struggles. The nobility opposed the broader-based forms of government that the merchants sought to promote, and the situation was aggravated by fierce inter-family feuds and continual raids on Florentine trade by 'robber barons'.

San Miniato's facade dates from the 11th century

To make matters worse, powerful foreign interests became involved. The pro-Pope Guelph and pro-Emperor Ghibelline parties *(see box opposite)*, which first developed in the 13th century, had their origins in other Italian cities, where the ambitions of the Papacy and the Holy Roman Empire (founded in AD962) were diverging dangerously. Further complicating matters was the French monarchy, which took an especially keen interest in Florentine developments, and was always ready to interfere in (and profit from) the internecine strife.

Other Tuscan cities soon followed suit with their own Guelph-Ghibelline factions, and Tuscany remained in a state of turmoil for more than two centuries. Pisa, Lucca, Pistoia, Siena, Arezzo and Florence became in turn enemies or allies, depending on which party held power in which town.

Social and Cultural Developments

Yet in spite of these setbacks, Florentine commerce and banking continued to develop, and its woollen-cloth trade prospered. The first gold *fiorino* was minted in the mid-13th century. With the city's patron St Giovanni on one side and the symbolic Florentine lily on the other, it was rapidly adopted throughout Europe as the standard unit of currency.

The city's social evolution during this time was also remarkable: organised 'factories', or workshops, were opened; hospitals, schools and charitable societies were founded; the university (one of Europe's oldest) turned out lawyers, teachers and doctors; streets were paved, and laws were passed regulating noise and nuisance; and the Brotherhood of the Misericordia, a forerunner of the Red Cross *(see page 31)*, was established. Although life was hard and Florence was never a democracy in the modern sense of the word, the city gave its citizens a unique feeling of belonging that overcame class or party differences.

In spite of their internal divisions, the Guelphs gradually edged the Ghibellines out of power. By the late 13th century, the bankers, merchants and city guilds had a firm grasp on the helm of the Florentine republic, and felt secure enough to turn their attention to the building of a fitting seat of government. Already involved with the construction of a sumptuous cathedral, a mighty palace of the people – the Palazzo del Popolo – was begun in 1298. This was later called the Palazzo della Signoria and is now known as the Palazzo Vecchio. Located in the Piazza della Signoria, it still serves

Pope vs Emperor

The names 'Guelph' (supporters of the Pope) and 'Ghibelline' (supporters of the Holy Roman Emperor) are said to come from the German Welf (dukes of Bavaria) and Waiblingen (the home of the Hohenstaufens) respectively.

as the city hall (after having followed a brief stint as a Medici residence during the Renaissance); it is one of the most handsome structures from this period still in existence.

The Dawn of a Golden Age

Florentine bankers now held the purse-strings of Europe, with agents in every major city. One group, headed by the Bardi and Peruzzi families, lent Edward III of England 1,365,000 gold florins to finance his campaigns against the French. Then in 1343 the double-dealing Edward suddenly declared himself bankrupt, and toppled the entire banking system.

As always, the resilient Florentines recovered, and the merchant interests set out with ruthless zeal to regain their lost prestige. Despite ceaseless social unrest, violent riots, disastrous floods, and the Black Death of 1347–8, which claimed over half the city's population (and one-third of Italy's), by the early 1400s Florence found itself stronger and richer than ever. The foundation had been laid for its brightest moment to come.

In addition to this commercial success, the city's cultural life was flourishing, moving towards the early years of what was to become known as the Renaissance. Interest in long-neglected Greek and Latin literature was being revived. While Florentine historians started recording their city's progress for posterity, merchant guilds and the nouveaux riches found time between business deals and party vendettas to indulge in artistic patronage.

Despite factional divisions, the Florentines were able to plan ambitious public works and awe-inspiring private palazzos: the Duomo, Giotto's Campanile, the great monastic churches of Santa Croce and Santa Maria Novella, the Bargello and the Palazzo Vecchio were all begun or completed during the tumultuous 14th century.

The power of the important business families, the *signori*, was slowly proving to be greater than that of the guilds. The ambitious Medici family of wealthy wool merchants and bankers came to dominate every facet of Florentine life for 60 golden years (1434–94) and, to a diminishing degree, the decades thereafter. The Medici were shrewd politicians and enthusiastic and discerning patrons of the arts. As patrons they led the city and its people to unparalleled heights of civilisation, at a time when most of Europe was struggling to free itself from the coarse, tangled mesh of medieval feudalism.

The Renaissance

The term 'Renaissance' *(Rinascimento)* was coined by 16th-century Florentine artist and historian Giorgio Vasari (1511–74), whose book *Lives of the Most Excellent Painters, Sculp-*

Artisans at work, depicted on the church of Orsanmichele

tors and Architects tells almost everything we know about the great Italian artists from the 13th century up to his own time (some historians believe the expression came into use much later). 'Renaissance' means 'rebirth', which is exactly how Vasari saw the events of the 15th century – the world appeared to be waking from a long sleep and taking up life where antiquity had left off. The Church had dominated the cultural life of Europe throughout the Middle Ages. Literature, architecture, painting, sculpture and music were all aimed at the glorification of God, rather than the celebration of earthly life and beauty. The Greek and Roman concept of 'art for art's sake' had been forgotten until it was revived in 15th-century Florence; a comparison of Cimabue's *Virgin Enthroned* (*c.*1290) with *La Primavera* by Botticelli (1477–8) illustrates the difference between the art of the Middle Ages and the Renaissance.

Resurrection of the Son of Theophilus by Filippino Lippi

The idea had taken hold that life must be lived to its fullest and that the pursuit of earthly knowledge, beauty and pleasure were what counted most in the brief time allotted to man. The arts and sciences of the Renaissance were directed towards those ends.

Lorenzo de' Medici

Poet, naturalist, art collector, dabbler in philosophy and architecture (an example of what is still referred to as a 'Renaissance man'), Lorenzo was perhaps the most outstanding member of the Medici dynasty.

The Medici

Although few of the early Medici ever held office in the city government, three of them were in fact the true rulers of Florence. They were: Cosimo, *Il Vecchio* ('the Elder', 1389–1464), a munificent patron of the arts and letters and founder of the Medici dynasty, who earned himself the title *pater patriae* ('father of his country'); his son, Piero, *Il Gottoso* ('the Gouty', 1416–69); and his grandson Lorenzo, *Il Magnifico* ('the Magnificent', 1449–92). Ably pulling strings via supporters elected to the republican government (the *Signoria*), all three were expert politicians who knew how to win the hearts and minds of the Florentine masses.

Lorenzo's diplomatic skill kept Italy temporarily free of wars and invasions, and his love of the arts had a direct effect on cultural life as we know it today. On Lorenzo's death in 1492, his son Piero lo Sfortunato (the Unfortunate) took his place. Loutish and devoid of taste, Piero was deemed unworthy of the Medici name; he lasted only two years. When Charles VIII of France invaded Italy, Piero first opposed him but suddenly changed sides as it became clear that the French were winning. He had to accept humiliating terms of settlement. The Florentine people were so enraged that they drove him from the city and set up a republic. It was at this time that Niccolò Machiavelli held office in Florence, gaining first-hand experience in the arts of intrigue and diplomacy.

Bonfire of the Vanities

The spiritual force behind the new republic was a fanatical Dominican friar from Ferrara, Girolamo Savonarola (1452–98). Prior of the Monastery of San Marco, he preached regularly in the Duomo during Lorenzo's last years. At first his message of the decadence of the Renaissance was ignored by Florentines. However, by 1490 audiences of thousands had heard him inveigh against the excesses of the Medici courts, prophesying apocalyptic punishments for the city if its people did not embrace a more godly way of life.

In 1494, he decreed the destruction of the 'vanities' of art, and Florentines flocked to the Piazza della Signoria with armfuls of illuminated books, hand-loomed textiles and precious paintings, which they hurled upon a huge bonfire in the middle of the square. Even Botticelli joined in, flinging some of his own paintings into the flames. But Savonarola

Florentine Explorers

Amerigo Vespucci (1454–1512) went down in history as the man who gave his name to America. Banker, businessman and navigator, he crossed the Atlantic in the wake of Christopher Columbus (who was from Genoa), and explored the coast of South America, discovering the estuaries of the Orinoco and Rio de la Plata. His main achievement was to ascertain that Columbus had, in fact, discovered a 'New World', and not Asia, as Columbus himself had maintained.

More than 20 years later, another Florentine navigator, Giovanni da Verrazzano (1485–1528), searching for the legendary Northwest Passage, sailed through the narrows that now bear his name, and discovered New York Harbour.

had powerful enemies (Pope Borgia, for one) who soon brought about his downfall. He was arrested, sentenced to death for heresy, and hanged and burned where his 'bonfire of the vanities' had taken place four years earlier; a bronze plaque still marks the spot in Piazza della Signoria.

Lorenzo de' Medici

In 1512, Piero's brothers, Giovanni and Giuliano, returned to Florence, putting an end to the republic. Expelled in 1527, the persistent Medici were back three years later, after an eight-month siege, with the help of the Holy Roman Emperor Charles V.

During the subsequent rule of Grand Duke Cosimo I de' Medici (1537–1574), an attempt was made to revive the spirit of the Medici's earlier golden age. Some of Florence's most prominent monuments date from this period, including the Santa Trinità Bridge, the Boboli Garden (Cosimo's back garden when residing in the Palazzo Pitti), the Neptune Fountain in the Piazza della Signoria, and Cellini's magnificent bronze *Perseus*, a copy of which stands in the Loggia dei Lanzi in Piazza della Signoria.

The 18th and 19th Centuries

Under the rule of the grand dukes of Tuscany (Medici until 1737, then Hapsburgs up to 1859), Florence sank into a torpor which lasted for more than three centuries. Anna Maria Ludovica, last of the Medici line, who died in 1749, made a grand final gesture worthy of her Renaissance forebears.

Farsightedly, she bequeathed the entire Medici art collection (the basis of the staggering collection of the Uffizi Gallery, formerly the offices of the Medici) to the city 'to attract foreigners', on condition that none of it ever be sold or removed from Florence. Her wish was granted, for the foreigners came, at first a small but steady trickle of privileged young gentlemen doing the Grand Tour of Europe, the traditional finishing touch to a gentleman's cultural education; though if truth be told, Italy's cultural treasures made little lasting impression on the majority of these visitors.

In the early 19th century, however, a new breed of traveller appeared – the 'Italianate Englishman', led by the poets Byron and Shelley, and followed later in the century by the Brownings, John Ruskin (although his major work was on Venice), and the Ruskin-inspired Pre-Raphaelites. Rapturous Britons, who were smitten by the mythologised and romantic image of Italy, toured or settled in droves, bringing in their wake French, German and Russian tourists, all referred to as 'the English' by the Florentines. Queen Victoria herself visited the city. Florence Nightingale was named after the city of her birth (there is a statue of her in the Santa Croce cloister); she would go on to make her mark in the Crimean War.

After the dramatic events of the Risorgimento, when the occupying Austrians were expelled, Florence had a brief moment of glory as the capital of the newly unified kingdom of Italy (1865–71). With the transfer of the capital to Rome, the story of Florence merges into Italian history.

Early 20th Century

Despite the excitement at the time of unification, the early years of independence were turbulent. Political crisis followed crisis, and governments became vunerable to attack from reactionary forces. During World War I, Italy fought against Germany and Austria, but afterwards the feeling that it had been insufficiently rewarded for its sacrifices was exploited by the fascist Benito Mussolini, who seized power in 1922 and declared himself prime minister of Italy.

World War II to the Present Day

With the Rome–Berlin Axis of 1937, Mussolini linked the fate of Italy to Hitler's Germany, dragging his country to defeat in World War II. The fascist government fell in 1943, and some of the most heroic battles of the Italian resistance were fought in and around Florence, which lay just to the

German paratroopers face Allied soldiers across the Arno

south of the 'Gothic Line'. The retreating Germans blew up all the bridges over the Arno except for the Ponte Vecchio, spared, it is believed, because of its famous past (this didn't stop the Germans from destroying the bridge-heads on either side, however). The city's art treasures and landmark architecture survived unscathed. Mussolini and his mistress came to a sticky end: they were executed in 1945 and their bodies displayed in Milan.

Since 1945 the city has also seen destruction on a large scale. On 4 November 1966 the Arno broke its banks, causing immense damage to many of the city's artworks and killing 35 people. And in 1993 a Mafia bomb exploded by the Uffizi, killing five people and damaging around 200 precious works of art *(see also pages 9–10)*.

Present-day Florence is a lively and important university city with a tradition of radical politics, attracting a huge number of international students. Also, because of its cultural heritage, it is a major tourist destination. The preservation of the city's cultural attractions can, however, present obstacles to much-needed infrastructure projects. The Nuovi Uffizi scheme, first mooted over 50 years ago, that hopes to relieve overcrowding and solve visitor-access problems, has been subject to severe delays due to concerns about how the new exit would fit into the surrounding fabric of the city. Similar objections were raised about the tram network that has been discussed for years but is only now getting under way.

One of the many faces of modern Florence

Historical Landmarks

8th century BC The first settlements on the site of Florence.

c.59BC The foundation of the Roman city of Florentia.

3rd century AD St Minias brings Christianity to Florence.

570 The Lombards take control of Tuscany.

774 Charlemagne defeats the Lombards and takes over Tuscany.

1001 Death of Marquese Ugo, who made Florence capital of Tuscany.

11th century Most of the city's churches rebuilt.

1115 Florence becomes a self-governing commune.

1215 Beginning of the civil strife between the Guelphs and Ghibellines.

1296–9 Work begins on the Duomo and Palazzo Vecchio.

1302 Dante expelled in a mass purge of Ghibellines.

1347–8 The Black Death kills over half of the city's population.

1400 onwards The beginning of the Renaissance and the rise of Florence as the pre-eminent cultural centre in Europe.

1434–64 Cosimo de' Medici rules Florence.

1469–92 The rule of Lorenzo 'the Magnificent'.

1494–8 Under the influence of Savonarola, the citizens declare Florence a republic under the rule of Christ.

1512 The Medici regain control of the city.

1537–74 The rule of Cosimo I; Florence goes into slow decline.

1610 Galileo made court mathematician to Cosimo II.

1737 The death of Gian Gastone, last Medici ruler of Florence.

1860 Tuscany becomes part of emerging United Kingdom of Italy.

1865–71 Florence is capital of the new kingdom.

1944 The retreating Germans destroy three bridges of the Arno.

1966 Florence is devastated by floods.

1988 Traffic is excluded from the historic centre.

1993 A Mafia bomb kills five people and damages the Uffizi.

2002 The euro replaces the Italian lira as the main unit of currency.

2004 Michelangelo's *David* is redisplayed after restoration.

2007 The Nuovi Uffizi project finally gets under way.

2008 The first lines of the city's new tram network are begun.

WHERE TO GO

Although Florence's suburbs spread far along the Arno Valley, the old part of the city with most of the sights of interest to visitors is compact and easy to negotiate on foot. On the northern bank of the River Arno is the *centro storico* (historic centre), laid out around three large squares. Around the edge of the *centro storico* are three of the city's most important churches, San Lorenzo, San Marco and Santa Maria Novella. Across the river is the district of Oltrarno. Settled later than the north bank, this was once an area of workshops and artisans and still retains a more laid-back air than the heavily touristed streets around the Duomo and Piazza della Signoria.

PIAZZA DEL DUOMO

The superb **Piazza del Duomo** is situated to the north of the grid of narrow streets that make up Florence's *centro storico*. At its centre, the magnificent cathedral is the symbolic heart of the city and remains its tallest building.

The Duomo

The huge multicoloured facade of the **Duomo** (Mon–Wed, Fri 10am–5pm, Thur 10am–3.30pm, Sat 10am–4.45pm, Sun 1.30–4.45pm; free; www.operaduomo.firenze.it) rises majestically alongside the pointed roof of the Baptistery. Officially known as Santa Maria dei Fiori (Saint Mary of the Flowers), the Duomo was designed by the great architect Arnolfo di Cambio (1245–1302), who was also responsible for the Palazzo Vecchio *(see pages 33–5)*, and was intended to surpass all the great buildings of antiquity in both size and splendour.

The Duomo's neo-Gothic facade was added in the 19th century

Work commenced around 1296 on the site of the far smaller 5th-century cathedral of Santa Reparata, but was not completed until the second half of the 15th century; the cathedral's wonderfully elaborate, neo-Gothic facade was added as late as the 19th century. Like the majority of Tuscan churches of the time, the Duomo presents a unique local version of Gothic-style architecture, that is not easily compared to other northern European ecclesiastical buildings of the same period.

The mighty **cupola** was the contribution of Filippo Brunelleschi (1377–1446), the first true 'Renaissance' architect, who was inspired by the dome on Rome's Pantheon, rebuilt for Emperor Hadrian in about AD125.

When the ambitious Florentines decided that their showpiece cathedral must have a great dome, they held a public competition in 1418. Brunelleschi submitted the winning design (encouraged by the organisers to make it *il più bello che si può* – as beautiful as possible) and, just as important, a workable building scheme. His original wooden model can be seen in the Museo dell'Opera del Duomo *(see page 32)*. In Florence, where beauty and art were never the preserve of the rich alone, these competitions used to cause immense, popular excitement. Citizens from all walks of life often sat together on the panel of judges.

Brunelleschi's magnificent dome, the first giant cupola since antiquity, was completed in 1436. It was visible for miles, dwarfing the red-tiled rooftops around it, and confirming the feeling of the day that nothing was beyond the science and ingenuity of man.

A long climb

You can climb up the spiralling 463 steps to the top of the lantern on the huge cupola and enjoy breathtaking panoramic views over the city. Entry to the steps is via the Porta della Mandoria (Mon–Fri 8.30am–7pm, Sat 8.30am–5pm) on the northern side of the Duomo.

The cathedral is Florence's tallest building at 107m (351ft)

By contrast with the polychrome exterior, the cathedral's **interior** is strikingly vast and stark. Although most of the original statuary was long ago moved to the Museo dell'Opera del Duomo, there are still some important works of art to be seen, such as the magnificent 16th-century fresco on the inside of the cupola. The depiction of *The Last Judgement* was begun by Giorgio Vasari and finished by his student Federico Zuccari.

Lorenzo Ghiberti's bronze shrine below the high altar was made to house the remains of St Zenobius, one of Florence's first bishops. The three stained-glass rose windows on the entrance wall were also designed by the versatile Ghiberti.

Left of the entrance are some unusual *trompe l'œil* frescoes of two 15th-century *condottieri* (mercenary captains) who fought for Florence. The right-hand one, painted by Paolo Uccello, the great master of perspective, commemorates an Englishman, John Hawkwood, the only foreigner ever buried in the Duomo, although his remains were later repatriated. Uccello is also responsible for the 1443 **ora ital-ica** clock next to Ghiberti's windows.

On the right, just inside the cathedral's entrance, are the steps down to the **crypt** (closed Sun, last entry 30 mins before closing; charge), which contains Brunelleschi's simple tomb.

The Campanile

The Duomo's free-standing **Campanile di Giotto** (daily 8.30am–7.30pm, last entry at 6.50pm; charge) is one of Florence's most graceful landmarks. The bell-tower was begun in 1334 by Giotto, and completed in 1359 by his successors Andrea Pisano and Andrea Talenti. Faced in green, white and pink marble to match the Duomo, the lowest storey bears hexagonal reliefs illustrating *Genesis* and various arts and industries by Pisano and Luca della Robbia. The niches in the second storey contain statues of the Prophets and Sibyls, some by Donatello. It's worth making the 414-step climb to the top for a bird's-eye view of the cathedral and a city that was never permitted to build higher than the cathedral's dome.

The Baptistery

Opposite the Duomo lies **Il Battistero** (Mon–Sat noon–7pm, Sun 8.30am–2pm; charge; www.operaduomo.firenze.it). Acclaimed as the oldest building in Florence, this precious gem of octagonal Romanesque architecture, built in the early part of the 12th century on what is believed to be the site of a Roman temple, served for a time as Florence's cathedral. With the exception of its doors, the exterior appearance remains as it was in the time of Dante. Brilliant 13th-century mosaics inside the cupola include scenes from the *Creation*, *Life of St John* and an 8m (26ft) Christ in the *Last Judgement*.

The Baptistery's principal claim to fame is its three sets of **gilded bronze doors** (now copies; originals in the Museo dell'Opera del Duomo). Those on the south side are the oldest. Dating from the 14th century, they are the work of Andrea Pisano. A competition to design another set of doors was held in 1401, financed by one of the merchant guilds. Brunelleschi was among those who submitted an entry, but Lorenzo Ghiberti's submission was declared the winner. Their original entries are now in the Bargello. The competition is now seen as an important landmark in the development of the Renaissance *(see page 41)*.

The first doors Ghiberti produced can be seen on the north side of the Baptistery. The artist later went on to make the magnificent east

Part of Ghiberti's gilded 'Gates of Paradise'

doors, facing the Duomo and therefore the most important, which were described by an admiring Michelangelo as being fit to be the 'Gates of Paradise'. The name has stuck ever since.

Loggia del Bigallo

On the corner of Via dei Calzaiuoli, south of the Baptistery, is the graceful 14th-century **Loggia del Bigallo** (Wed–Mon 10am–6pm; charge), once part of the headquarters of a society for the care of orphans and now a small museum with some fine works of art. Across the street lie the headquarters of one of Florence's oldest and most respected social institutions, the **Brotherhood of the Misericordia**. Founded by St

An encounter in the Museo dell'Opera del Duomo

Peter Martyr in 1244, it was especially needed during frequent bouts of pestilence and plague. Today's unpaid volunteers, easily recognised in their black hooded capes, provide free assistance to the poor and needy, and also run an ambulance service.

Museo dell'Opera del Duomo

At the east end of the piazza, the **Museo dell'Opera del Duomo** (Mon–Sat 9am–7.30pm, Sun 9am–1.45pm; charge; www.operaduomo. firenze.it) holds many of the Duomo's most precious treasures and original sculptures. Highlights include the original door panels from the Baptistery; a sumptuous 14th–15th-century silver-faced altar from the Baptistery; rich gold and silver reliquaries (one of which houses the index finger of St John, Florence's patron saint); Brunelleschi's original wooden model of the Duomo's cupola; Donatello's harrowing wooden effigy of Mary Magdalene and the *Zuccone* that once graced the Campanile; and two beautiful sculptured choir lofts *(cantorie)*, one by Donatello and the other by Luca della Robbia. The museum also houses Michelangelo's unfinished *Pietà*, which is said to have been intended for his own tomb.

Via dell'Oriuolo leads to the **Museo Firenze com'era** (Fri–Wed 9am–2pm; charge), where you will find a great number of maps, paintings, prints and photographs illustrating the history of the city.

PIAZZA DELLA SIGNORIA

The second major square of the *centro storico* is **Piazza della Signoria**. If the Piazza del Duomo is the religious heart of Florence, this piazza is its political and social counterpart. The city rulers have gathered here since the 13th century, and the present-day offices of the city council are still housed in the austere Palazzo Vecchio.

Palazzo Vecchio

Dominating the square is the fortress-like **Palazzo Vecchio** (Fri–Wed 9am–7pm, Thur 9am–2pm; charge), also known as the Palazzo della Signoria after the highest tier of the city's 15th-century government, the *Signoria*, which convened here. Designed in 1299 by Arnolfo di Cambio, who also designed the Duomo, it was intended to house the city's government. After serving briefly as a Medici residence, it acquired the name Palazzo Vecchio (Old Palace) in 1550 when the Medici moved their headquarters over the river to the new Palazzo Pitti *(see page 69)*. The palazzo's off-centre 94m (308ft) tower, added in 1310, helps to soften the squareness of the palazzo, and complements its off-centre position on the piazza.

The imposing Palazzo Vecchio

The palazzo's interior comes as a surprise after the medieval austerity of the exterior. It was completely remodelled when Cosimo I de' Medici moved into it in 1540. The **courtyard**, designed by Michelozzi Michelozzo in 1453, is delightful. The ornate stucco and frescoes were added in 1565 by Vasari, who also designed the fountain at the centre. Verrocchio's bronze fountainhead depicting a putto with a dolphin was brought here from Lorenzo de' Medici's villa at Careggi. What you see here is a copy; the original is displayed upstairs.

The palazzo's highlights include the massive **Salone dei Cinquecento**, on the first floor. Built to house the parliament of the short-lived Florentine republic declared in 1494 *(see page 20)*, it was turned into a grand throne room by Cosimo I, and decorated with giant Vasari frescoes of Florentine victories and Michelangelo's statue *The Genius of Victory,* representing Cosimo's triumph over enemy Siena in 1554–5. Three centuries later, the first parliament of a united Italy met here. It is still used today for special government functions.

A small door to the right of the main entrance leads into the **Studiolo di Francesco I** (only accessible on a guided tour), a little gem of a study designed by Vasari. It is covered from floor to barrel-vaulted ceiling with painted allegorical panels (representing *Fire*, *Water*, *Earth* and *Air*), and two Bronzino portraits of Cosimo I and his consort gazing down haughtily.

Across the hall, another door leads into the **Quartiere di Leone X**, the apartments of the first Medici pope. The rooms are sumptuously decorated with frescoes celebrating the achievements of the Medici family. Stairs lead up to the equally sumptuous **Quartiere degli Elementi**, with painted allegories on the theme of the elements. The Terraza di Saturno at the back provides a fine view across the river.

A gallery above the Salone dei Cinquecento leads to the **Quartiere di Eleonora** (the apartments of Cosimo I's Spanish wife), a riot of gilt, painted ceilings and rich furnishings.

The palazzo's inner courtyard, designed by Michelozzo in 1453

The splendid 15th-century **Sala dei Gigli** (Hall of the Lilies), all blue and gold, is lavishly decorated with Florentine heraldry, a gilt-panelled ceiling, bright Ghirlandaio frescoes, and superb doors inlaid with figures of Dante and Petrarch. Here stands Donatello's original bronze of *Judith and Holofernes* (a copy is in the piazza outside).

Next door is the splendid **Sala Mappamondo**, a cupboard-lined room whose wooden panels were painted with maps by two learned Dominican friars (1563–87). The 57 maps illustrate the extent of the world known to the West in the late 16th century.

Loggia dei Lanzi

On the south side of the Piazza della Signoria is the Loggia della Signoria, more commonly known as the **Loggia dei Lanzi,** built in the late 14th century. Originally a covered vantage point for city officials at public ceremonies, it took its later name from Cosimo I's Swiss-German mercenary bodyguards, known as *Landsknechts* (Italianised to *Lanzichenecchi*), who used it as a guardroom during his nine-year residence in the Palazzo Vecchio. Since the late 18th century the loggia has been used as an open-air sculpture museum, but celebrated works of art have been displayed here since long before then. Cellini's fine bronze *Perseus* was originally placed here, on Cosimo's order in 1554. Giambologna's famous *Rape of the Sabine Women* was added in 1583, while his *Hercules and the Centaur* and the Roman statues at the back, donated by the Medici, were added towards the end of the 18th century.

Giambologna's *Rape of the Sabine Women*

In front of the palazzo a *marzocco* – a heraldic lion bearing the city's arms (the symbol of Florence) – has graced the piazza for almost as long as the palazzo itself (what you see today is a copy; the original is in the Bargello). Michelangelo's *David* was positioned here in 1504 as a republican symbol but was moved to the Accademia *(see page 60)* in 1873 and replaced by a copy (the present version is an early 20th-century copy; a bronze version can be found across the river in the Piazzale Michelangelo). The rather grotesque statue of *Hercules and Cacus* beside *David* is the work of a 16th-century sculptor, Bandinelli.

The Uffizi

Between the Palazzo Vecchio and the Arno, the **Galleria degli Uffizi** (Uffizi Gallery; Tue–Sun 8.15am–6.50pm; charge; www.polomuseale. firenze.it) stretches down either side of the narrow Piazzale degli Uffizi. Built by Vasari in the second half of the 16th century – it would be his greatest architectural work – the building was in-

Crowds gather outside the Uffizi

tended to house the headquarters of the various government offices (*uffizi* is Old Italian for 'offices'), the official mint and workshops for Medici craftsmen. It is now the home of one of the world's most famous and important art galleries.

There are usually long queues to get in, and the gallery can be very crowded. Although it costs a little more, to avoid the queues it is wise to book a timed entrance ticket in advance by contacting Firenze Musei (tel: 055-294 883; www.b-ticket. com/b-ticket/uffizi). To try to improve problems of access and overcrowding, the ongoing Nuovi Uffizi project (www. nuoviuffizi.it) will create a new entrance area and aims to double the exhibition space available by opening new areas of the building to the public. Some ideas, however, have not been without controversy, especially the design for a new exit by the Japanese architect Arata Isozaki.

Exhibited in chronological order, the paintings comprise the cream of Italian and European art from the 13th to 18th centuries. Begun by Cosimo I and added to by his successors, the collection was bequeathed to the people of Florence in perpetuity in 1737 by Anna Maria Ludovica, the last of the Medici dynasty, on condition that it never leave the city.

The first rooms contain those early Tuscan greats, **Cimabue** and **Giotto**. In their altarpieces depicting enthroned Madonnas (painted in 1280 and 1310, respectively), the mosaic-like stiffness of Cimabue's work contrasts vividly with Giotto's innovative depth and more expressive figures. One of the greatest painters of the 14th-century Sienese school was **Simone Martini**. This claim is evidenced by his graceful *Annunciation* (1333), painted for Siena's cathedral. Of the later Italian Gothic masterpieces, Gentile da Fabriano's *Adoration of the Magi* (1423) is the most exquisite. Of the early Renaissance works, do not miss Uccello's large and exciting depiction of the *Battle of San Romano* (1456), or the paintings by Masaccio.

Among the best-loved and most reproduced of Renaissance paintings are **Botticelli's** haunting *La Primavera* (The Allegory of Springtime; *c.*1480) and his renowned *Birth of Venus* (commonly referred to as 'Venus on the Half-Shell', *c.*1485). Botticelli's lifelike but theatrical *Adoration of the Magi* features portraits of the Medici family – Cosimo Il Vec-

Artistic Precedents

The lead-up to the great artistic breakthroughs of the Renaissance starts in the 13th and early 14th centuries. Influenced by the developments of the painter Cavallini in Rome, it was Giovanni Cimabue (1240–1302) who moved away from the static Byzantine tradition to found the Florentine school of painting, but it was the naturalism of his student Giotto (1266–1337) that made Florence the first city of Italian art, even if much of his best surviving work is in Padua.

In sculpture it was the work of father and son Nicola and Giovanni Pisano (*c.*1220–78 and *c.*1250–1314 respectively), with their pulpits for the churches of Pisa and Pistoia, who brought a greater realism to their work. Along with Andrea Pisano (no relation) and Arnolfo di Cambio, they laid the path for the ground-breaking work that would follow.

Detail of Botticelli's *Birth of Venus*

chio, his son Piero Il Gottoso and grandsons Lorenzo Il Magnifico and Giuliano (standing smugly on the extreme left, a few years before his murder). Botticelli himself, in a yellow cloak and golden curls, gazes out on the far right.

In the same room is an outstanding 15th-century Flemish painting – **Hugo Van der Goes's** huge triptych, *The Adoration of the Shepherds* (1478), which was painted for the Medici's Flemish agent, Tommaso Portinari. The Portinari family is immortalised on its side-panels. In a sunnier, lighter vein is **Ghirlandaio's** *Adoration* (1487).

The following room is devoted to **Leonardo da Vinci**. *The Baptism of Christ* (*c.*1474–5) was mostly the work of his great teacher, Verrocchio. Although only the background and the angel on the left were the work of the 18-year-old Leonardo, when Verrocchio saw how exquisitely his pupil had rendered the angel, he swore never to touch a paintbrush again. The *Annunciation* (1475) is entirely Leonardo's work,

Michelangelo's *Doni Tondo*

as is the *Adoration of the Magi* (1482). The latter is not just unfinished, but barely begun, sketched out in preparatory chiaroscuro, or light and shade, but gives insight into Leonardo's unique approach to the subject.

The **Tribuna** is an octagonal room, commissioned by the Medici from Buontalenti, which symbolises the four elements. The sumptuous 17th-century inlaid stone table, specially made for the room, took 16 years to complete. Here are **Bronzino's** portraits of Cosimo I's Spanish wife, *Eleonora of Toledo*, and their chubby, smiling baby son, *Giovanni*, one of the most famous child portraits ever painted.

Among the German masterpieces in the Uffizi, look out for **Dürer's** *Portrait of His Father* (1490) and *Adoration of the Magi* (1504), and **Cranach's** lifelike little portraits of Luther, his renegade wife, and a solid *Adam and Eve* (1526). Among the works of the 15th-century Venetian School are **Bellini's** strange, dream-like *Sacred Allegory*, painted about 1490 (its allegorical significance has never been fully explained).

The Uffizi contains just one work by the great **Michelangelo**, a round oil painting showing the Holy Family, known as the *Doni Tondo* (1503–5). Firmly but humanly treated, it is the only known panel painting by the artist better-known for frescoes and sculpture. Equally notable are **Raphael's** maternal *Madonna del Cardellino* (Madonna of the Goldfinch; c.1505) and a wistful self-portrait painted in Florence when he was only 23. The works by **Titian** include *Flora* (c.1515) and his celebrated, voluptuous nude, the *Venus of Urbino* (1538). The final room on this floor is dedicated to works by **Rembrandt**, including his famous *Portrait of an Old Man* (1665), as well as two wonderful self-portraits.

On the floor below there are five more rooms, one of which is given over to the works of **Caravaggio**, where you can see his splendidly decadent *Young Bacchus* (1589) and the *Sacrifice of Isaac* (1601–2).

Renaissance Artists

Although the glimmerings of humanism can be seen in works of Cimabue and Giotto, the Renaissance is said to have truly arrived when Brunelleschi submitted his design for the Baptistery doors in 1401. Although beaten by Ghiberti in the competition, Brunelleschi's relief of Abraham and Isaac is more dynamic and depicts the human drama of the story. Brunelleschi's most lasting legacy to the city is in architecture, especially his Duomo, Spedale degli Innocenti and the Pazzi Chapel, but he is also credited with the invention of measured perspective.

In sculpture, pride of place goes to Brunelleschi's friend Donatello (1386–1466), whose bas-relief on the plinth of his *St George* at Orsanmichele shows early use of perspective, and whose *David* was the first free-standing male nude since antiquity.

In painting, the Renaissance was ushered in by Masaccio (1401–28), with his solid modelled human figures, followed by Paolo Uccello (1397–1475), master of perspective, and the melancholic Filippo Lippi (1406–69). In the realm of religious art, the outstanding figures were Andrea Verrocchio (1435–88), Leonardo da Vinci's teacher and a fine sculptor, Domenico Ghirlandaio (1449–94), famous for his frescoes, and the exquisitely lyrical Botticelli (1444–1510). The High Renaissance saw the arrival of three master artists who epitomise the period: Leonardo da Vinci (1452–1519) – artist and scientist – Michelangelo (1475–1564) – sculptor, architect, painter and poet – and the exquisite paintings of Raphael (1483–1520).

Vasari Corridor

The Corridoio Vasariano is a graceful covered walkway built by Vasari in 1565, running from the Uffizi and over the Ponte Vecchio to the Medici's new headquarters in the Palazzo Pitti. It allowed Grand Duke Cosimo de' Medici to commute between the two without ever braving the elements or brushing shoulders with the populace. The corridor and its collection of portraits of artists can only be visited on certain days as part of a pre-booked tour (tel: 055-265 4321; charge), and the numbers of visitors allowed is very restricted.

Science Museum

The **Museo di Storia della Scienza** is a welcome change after over-indulgence in the arts. Renaissance Florence was an important centre of scientific research, and Cosimo II hired the best mathematicians, astronomers and cartographers from all over Europe and the Middle East. Their beautifully engraved astrolabes and armillary spheres, showing the motion of the heavenly bodies, are displayed here, alongside mahogany-and-brass reconstructions of Galileo's experiments and fascinating 15th- and 16th-century maps and globes that show how rapidly new discoveries were revolutionising our understanding of the world.

THE BARGELLO AND SANTA CROCE

East of Piazza della Signoria is **Piazza San Firenze**, a small square dominated by the towering Baroque facade of **San Firenze**, the seat of Florence's Law Courts.

The Bargello

On the northern edge of the square is the forbidding, fortress-like Palazzo del Bargello, home of the **Museo Nazionale del Bargello** (daily 8.15am–1.50pm, closed 2nd and 4th Mon, and 1st, 3rd and 5th Sun of month; charge; www.polomuseale.

firenze.com). Florence's original town hall and one of its earliest public buildings (begun around 1250), the Bargello served as the seat of the magistrates *(podestà)* responsible for law and order, and later housed the office of the Captain of Justice *(bargello)*, the 16th-century equivalent of today's police commissioner. Today, the Bargello is to sculpture what the Uffizi is to painting, for it houses many Renaissance masterpieces.

The first room beyond the entrance is the **Sala Michelangelo**, where marks on the wall record the water level of the 1966 flood at 3m (9ft). Michelangelo was only 21 when he finished his early masterpiece, *The Drunken Bacchus*. He sculpted the marble *Pitti Tondo* of the Virgin and Child eight years later, in 1504, while working on his famous *David* (now in the Accademia). You will also find Michelangelo's 'other David', aka *Apollo*, sculpted 30 years after the original.

Shopping in Piazza San Firenze

A door leads into the attractive courtyard, softened by the brownish hues of its *pietra forte*, and covered with a mélange of stone plaques bearing the arms of successive *podestà*. A 14th-century stone staircase leads to an arcaded loggia on the first floor, where you'll see Giambologna's series of remarkably lifelike bronze birds surrounding a marble figure representing *Architecture*.

The first-floor exhibits include Italian and Tuscan

ceramics, old Murano glass, French Limoges enamels and astonishing, delicate engraved seashells. The 14th-century chapel contains frescoes painted by a pupil of Giotto (the man behind the kneeling figure on the right is said to be Dante).

If you are pressed for time, head straight for the **Salone di Donatello**, which contains works by the sculptor that capture the spirit of early Renaissance Florence. Donatello's movingly human *St George* (1416) dominates the back wall of this impressively high-vaulted room. Commissioned by the armourers' guild as their contribution to the exterior decorations of Orsanmichele *(see page 52)*, its depth and sense of movement are generally believed to represent the first great sculptural achievement of the Renaissance.

Donatello's most important work – his bronze *David* (1440–50) – is credited as the first free-standing nude statue of the Renaissance. In contrast to the 'modern' feeling of *St George,* the *David* has an antique and ambiguous sensuality about it, while the delightful bronze *Amore* (Cupid) is positively Roman in style. More personal and dramatic are the two marble versions of *St John the Baptist*.

Be sure to take a look at Ghiberti's and Brunelleschi's original bronze panels *(The Sacrifice of Abraham)* for the Baptistery design competition of 1401 *(see page 31)*; they're on the right wall towards the back of the room.

The Sala di Verrocchio on the second floor has Verrocchio's bronze *David* (*c*.1471), which is said to have been modelled on the sculptor's 19-year-old pupil, Leonardo da Vinci. Also on the second floor is the model for Giambologna's *Rape of the Sabine Women* in the Loggia dei Lanzi.

Badia Fiorentina

Across the street from the Bargello is the church known as the **Badia Fiorentina** (entrance on Via Dante Alighieri; Mon 3–6pm), with its graceful bell-tower, part Romanesque, part

Gothic. Go inside for a moment to admire Filippino Lippi's delightful *Madonna Appearing to St Bernard*, on the left of the church as you enter.

From the southern end of Piazza San Firenze, take the Borgo dei Greci. This crosses **Via de' Bentaccordi**, one of the few curved streets in medieval Florence. It owes its shape to the fact that it once ran round the outside of Florence's Roman amphitheatre. At the far end of Borgo dei Greci you can see the black-and-white facade of Santa Croce.

Piazza Santa Croce

In what is a mostly residential neighbourhood today, the vast expanse of **Piazza Santa Croce** formed one of the social and political hubs of Renaissance Florence. Lorenzo and Giuliano de' Medici used to stage lavish jousts here, and defiant Florentines turned out in force during the 1530 siege to watch

Santa Croce's neo-Gothic facade

or take part in their traditional football game (re-enacted here every summer; *see Calendar of Events, page 95*). The buildings on the right-hand side of the square, with their cantilevered upper floors, were typical of the late medieval city.

The cavernous Franciscan church of **Santa Croce** (Mon–Sat 9.30am–5.30pm, Sun 1–5.30pm, last entry 30 mins before closing; charge, combined ticked with Museo dell'Opera di Santa Croce; www.santacroce.firenze.it) started off in 1210 as a modest chapel, situated in the middle of a working-class district. Arnolfo di Cambio, the architect of the Palazzo Vecchio and the Duomo, drew up the plans for a larger church, which was completed in the 14th century. The interior, beneath its open roof-beams, is grandly Gothic, while the facade is 19th-century neo-Gothic.

The church is the last resting place of some of the most illustrious figures in Italian history, many of them born in Tuscany. Just inside the door on the right is the **tomb of**

Dante

Dante Alighieri, the father of Italian literature, was born in Florence around 1265. As a consequence of his Guelph allegiances *(see pages 14–15)*, he was exiled from Florence for the last 19 years of his life and threatened with death by burning if he returned to the city. Though this sentence was repealed in 2008, his body remains in Ravenna and his tomb in Santa Croce lies empty.

His immortal poetic work, *The Divine Comedy*, describing a journey through Hell and Purgatory to arrive at last in Paradise, is one of the great landmarks of world literature. In it he juxtaposes divinely ordained political and social order with the ugly reality of the corrupt society around him. Dante was the first to write his masterpiece not in the usual scholarly Latin, but in his everyday language, thus establishing the Tuscan vernacular as the 'pure Italian' spoken today and used as the language of literature.

Michelangelo, designed by his first biographer, the 16th-century artist and architect Giorgio Vasari. The seated figures on the monument represent, from left to right, *Painting*, *Sculpture* and *Architecture*.

A statue of Dante outside Santa Croce; his empty tomb is within

The next tomb on the right wall, that of Florentine Dante Alighieri, lies empty, much to the dismay of Florence (he was exiled for political reasons). His body lies in Ravenna, where he died; the city has never given in to Florentine pleas for its return (a statue to him stands just outside Santa Croce's main entrance). Farther along is the tomb of Niccolò Machiavelli (1469–1527), civil servant, political theorist, historian and playwright. Gioacchino Rossini (1792–1868), Florentine by adoption and the composer of *The Barber of Seville* and *The William Tell Overture*, is also buried here.

Opposite Michelangelo is the tomb of Pisan Galileo Galilei (1564–1642), shown holding the telescope, which he invented. A plaque on the front of the tomb depicts the four moons of Jupiter which he discovered with the use of the instrument. On the same side of the church, beside the fourth column from the door, lies sculptor Lorenzo Ghiberti, creator of the famous Baptistery doors *(see page 31)*.

A tranquil chapel in the left transept houses a coloured wooden Christ on the cross carved by Donatello. His friend Brunelleschi mockingly dismissed the sculpture as 'a peasant on the cross' (Brunelleschi's answer can be found hanging in the Church of Santa Maria Novella). The honeycomb of family chapels on either side of the high altar contains a wealth of frescoes dating from the 14th to 16th centuries. To the right of the altar, in the **Bardi Chapel,** you'll find Giotto's finest and arguably most moving works – scenes from the life of St Francis, painted around 1320. The adjoining chapel contains Giotto frescoes of the life of St John, which were commissioned by the Peruzzi – rich bankers who donated most of the money for the church's imposing sacristy, where a fragment of St Francis's tunic is displayed.

Cappella dei Pazzi

The **Museo dell'Opera di Santa Croce** and, opposite, the **Cappella dei Pazzi** (same times as the church) are also of interest. The once-tarnished reputation of the Pazzi family (resulting from the assassination of Giuliano Medici in the

Giotto's *Life of St Francis* in the Bardi Chapel

Duomo) is more than redeemed by the latter, a small, exquisite chapel. One of the earliest and most important Renaissance religious interiors, it was designed for the Pazzi family by Brunelleschi in 1443, and contains his glazed-terracotta decorations of the four Evangelists and the tondos of the 12 Apostles by Luca della Robbia. The former refectory houses a museum containing frescoes and statues that were removed from the church for preservation, but its greatest treasure is Cimabue's massive 13th-century painted crucifix. Restored after near-destruction by the 1966 flood, it hangs by heavy cables that can raise it out of harm's way at the push of a button.

Casa Buonarroti

There are two more interesting museums close to Santa Croce. The **Casa Buonarroti** (Wed–Mon 9.30am–2pm; charge; www.casabuonarroti.it), at Via Ghibellina 70, was bought by Michelangelo with intentions of leaving it to his heirs. He lived for a short period of time in one of three small houses eventually combined to create this current residence. It contains letters, drawings and portraits of the great man, as well as a collection of 17th-century paintings illustrating his long, productive life. The exhibits include his famous sculptured relief the *Madonna of the Staircase*, completed before the artist was 16. His astonishing *Battle of the Lapiths and Centaurs* dates from around the same time.

The Horne Museum

Situated near the river at Via de' Benci 6, the **Museo della Fondazione Horne** (Mon–Sat 9am–1pm; charge; www.museohorne.it) is a superb little 15th-century palazzo, restored, briefly lived in, and eventually bequeathed to the city of Florence in 1916 by Englishman H.P. Horne. On display is his priceless collection of paintings, drawings, sculptures, ceramics, furniture, coins and old household utensils.

Piazza della Republica, once the site of the Roman forum

PIAZZA DELLA REPUBBLICA

To the west of Piazza della Signoria is the third major square of the *centro storico*, the grand **Piazza della Repubblica**, on the site of the old Roman forum. A jumble of medieval buildings was cleared during the 19th century to create the square, as part of the project to create a modern city that would be a fitting capital for the newly independent state of Italy. (Florence was capital of Italy in 1865–71, after which the capital was transferred to Rome). The piazza's stylish cafés fill up at lunchtime with office workers from the surrounding banks and businesses, and there's usually live music on summer evenings.

If you leave Piazza della Repubblica by Via degli Strozzi, just before the end of the street, on the left, you will see the massive walls of the **Palazzo Strozzi** (daily 10.30am–8.30pm; charge; www.palazzostrozzi.org), begun in 1489 as a private residence. Wrought-iron torch holders and rings for tethering horses are set in the masonry, but the cornice above the street remains unfinished (along with other details), since money for construction ran out after the death of Filippo Strozzi.

Via Tornabuoni and Piazza Santa Trinità

Via degli Strozzi leads to **Via Tornabuoni**, one of Florence's main shopping streets, lined with the boutiques of the city's fashion houses. At the southern end of the road is the **Piazza Santa Trinità**. On the western side of the piazza is the fine 16th-century facade of the church of **Santa Trinità** (daily 7am–noon, 4–7pm) by Bernardo Buontalenti. The Gothic interior comes as a complete surprise. It was built between the 13th and 15th centuries on the site of an older Romanesque church, the remains of which are still visible. Look for the late 15th-century Sassetti Chapel (second on the right from the chancel), with scenes from the life of St Francis by Ghirlandaio.

Outside the church, in the centre of the piazza, is the **Colonna della Giustizia** (Column of Justice), a granite pillar taken from the Baths of Caracalla in Rome. It was erected by Grand Duke Cosimo I de' Medici to celebrate his victory over a band of exiled Florentines anxious to overthrow him and re-establish a more democratic government.

Many wealthy families lived in the area, building impressive palazzos and sponsoring richly frescoed chapels. The exquisite, early 16th-century **Palazzo Bartolini-Salimbeni** and the 13th-century fortress-like **Palazzo Spini-Feroni** both stand on the piazza. The latter has been unofficially renamed the Palazzo Ferragamo, after the local family whose expanding empire of fashion and style is now located within the palazzo; its street-level retail store is one of the area's most alluring. Above the shop is the **Museo Ferragamo** (Sept–July Mon–Fri 9am–1pm, 2–6pm by appointment only; www.salvatoreferragamo.it), which has an exhibition on the life and work of the famous shoemaker.

Shopping for souvenirs in the Mercato Nuovo

Palazzo Davanzati and Mercato Nuovo

East of Piazza Santa Trinità, on Via Porta Rossa, is the **Palaz-zo Davanzati** (daily 8.15am–1.50pm, closed 2nd and 4th Sun, 1st, 3rd and 5th Mon of the month; www.polomuseale. firenze.it). Although this 14th-century palace presents a stern exterior, the rooms are full of colour. Everything, including toilets and kitchens, has been preserved in period style.

Via Porta Rossa leads on to the **Mercato Nuovo**. A market has existed here since the 11th century, and the current arcade was built in 1547–51 for the sale of silk and gold. The main attraction here is the profusion of stalls selling bags, belts, small leather goods and assorted souvenirs.

Orsanmichele

North of the market, on Via della Calzaiuoli, is the unusual church of **Orsanmichele** (Tue–Fri 10am–5pm, Sat–Sun 10am–6.30pm). The original building was an open-sided loggia, like the Mercato Nuovo, and was rebuilt in 1337 by the silk guild for use as a market. It was converted to a church in 1380, and in the early 15th century the two upper storeys were added and used as an emergency granary (in the rear left-hand corner of the ceiling you can see the ducts through which grain was poured). Mystical and mysterious, the pillared interior is dominated by Orcagna's splendid 14th-century altarpiece, built around an allegedly miracle-working image of the Madonna.

Adopted by the city's wealthy merchant and craft guilds, the church's square, fortress-like exterior was embellished with Gothic-style niches and statues during the late 14th and early 15th centuries. Each guild paid for one of the 14 niches and commissioned a statue of its patron or favourite saint.

On the north side of the church is a copy of Donatello's *St George* (the original is in the Bargello). Commissioned by the armourers' and sword-makers' guild, this work was one of the first masterpieces of Renaissance sculpture. Particularly revolutionary at the time was the relief underneath the statue of St George killing the dragon.

Copies of Ghiberti's statues of *St Matthew* and *St Stephen* can be seen on the west side, opposite the impressive 13th-century **Palazzo dell' Arte della Lana**, once the headquarters of the powerful wool merchants' guild.

A lucky pig

To the south of the Mercato Nuovo is *Il Porcellino*, a 17th-century bronze statue of a boar, copied from a Roman marble original now in the Uffizi. Legend has it that if you stroke his nose and toss a coin into the fountain, you will return to the city.

SAN LORENZO

This area to the north of the Duomo was home to the Medici
dynasty for centuries and is the final resting place of all of
the family's most important figures.

The rough, unfaced stone facade of **San Lorenzo** (Mon–
Fri 10am–5pm, Sun Mar–Oct only 1.30–5pm; charge; www.
operamedicealaurenziana.it) looks for all the world like a
huge Tuscan barn. Financed by the Medici, the prestigious
project was built by Brunelleschi between 1425 and 1446,
with its facade to have been completed by Michelangelo. It
never was, but the artist's model is on display at the Casa
Buonarroti museum. For once at least, 19th-century architects did not try to finish the job.

Florence's first entirely Renaissance church and one of Filippo Brunelleschi's earliest architectural triumphs (before he
built the Duomo's cupola), the building was begun on the site
of a 4th-century basilica. Cosimo Il Vecchio later had his
palace built within sight of the church (the Palazzo Medici-
Riccardi, with its entrance on Via Cavour). He liked to consider the Church of San Lorenzo as the Medici's parish church.

A door in the left wall of the church leads to the cloister
and the stairs up to the **Biblioteca Medicea Laurenziana**
(Laurentian Library, also accessible by a door to the left of
the front entrance to the church; Sun–Fri 9.30am–1.30pm;
charge; www.bml.firenze.sbn.it), one of Michelangelo's architectural masterpieces. A monumental staircase climbs to
the reading room, graced with a splendid wooden ceiling and
earthy terracotta floor. Commissioned by Pope Clement VII
in 1524 to house a precious collection of Medici books and
manuscripts, and opened to the public in 1571, it's regarded as one of the world's most beautiful libraries.

The sober church of San Lorenzo was the burial site of many
of the Medici. Cosimo Il Vecchio himself is in the crypt beneath

A splendid fresco inside San Lorenzo's dome

the dome, while his parents are in the Old Sacristy, along with his two sons, Piero Il Gottoso and Giovanni, in a sumptuous porphyry-and-bronze tomb by Verrocchio. That giant of early Renaissance art, Donatello (who decorated the Brunelleschi-designed Old Sacristy), is buried in the left transept.

The Medici Chapels

San Lorenzo is best-known and most visited for the far more sumptuous Medici tombs, found in the **Cappelle Medicee** (Medici Chapels; daily 8.15am–1.50pm, closed 2nd and 4th Sun, 1st, 3rd and 5th Mon of the month; charge). To visit them, you must go outside and walk around to the opposite end of the church, where you will find the entrance in Piazza Madonna degli Aldobrandini amid a jumble of stalls from the daily outdoor tourist market. From the crypt, filled with the tombs of minor family members, a staircase leads up to the **Cappella dei Principi** (the Chapel of the Princes). This early 17th-century Baroque extravaganza (added on after the completion of the New Sacristy; *see below*) was intended to be the family burial vault to surpass all others. The workmanship of multi-coloured inlaid marble and semi-precious stones is astounding, even if by today's standards it looks a little over-the-top. Six huge sarcophagi bear the mortal remains of some lesser-known Medici (left to right from the entrance): Cosimo III, Francesco I, Cosimo I, Ferdinando I, Cosimo II and Ferdinando II.

Follow the stream of visitors to the main attraction, the **New Sacristy** *(Sagrestia Nuova)*, reached via a corridor beside the stairs. This is an amazing one-man show by Michelangelo, who spent more than 14 years designing the interior and creating seven of the sculptures. Commissioned in 1520 by the future Pope Clement VII (the illegitimate son of Giuliano de' Medici) as a resting place for both his father (killed in the Duomo during the Pazzi conspiracy) and uncle (Lorenzo Il Magnifico), it also accommodates two recently deceased cousins (Giuliano, Duke of Nemours, and Lorenzo II, Duke of Urbino). The fore-shortened effect of the upper windows gives the cupola a feeling of still greater height. The walls behind the altar bear architectural sketches and markings, some of which are attributed to Michelangelo himself. Michelangelo worked on the Sacristy from 1521 to 1534; it was finished by Vasari in 1556.

The two more illustrious members of the Medici clan are buried to the right of the entrance, beneath Michelangelo's fine *Virgin and Child*, which is flanked by figures of the Medici patron saints, Cosmas and Damian. But it is the two undistinguished cousins, ironically enough, who have been immortalised by Michelangelo with two of the most famous funeral monuments of all time. On the right stands an idealised, war-like Giuliano, Duke of Nemours, above two splendid figures symbolising *Night* (female) and *Day* (male), reclining on the elegantly curved sarcophagus. The unfinished face of *Day* (on the right), with the visible marks of Michelangelo's chisel, makes the figure all the more remarkable. *Night* is accompanied by the symbols of darkness – an owl, a mask, the moon, and a sack of opium symbolising sleep. Opposite, a pensive Lorenzo, Duke of Urbino, sits above *Dawn* (female) and *Dusk* (male).

The Mercato Centrale and Palazzo Riccardi

Just north of here, visit the busy, leather-scented street market of Via dell'Ariento and the late 19th-century covered **Mercato Centrale** for a dose of local colour.

Michelangelo's *Night*

East of San Lorenzo on Via Cavour is the massive **Palazzo Medici-Riccardi** (entrance on Via Cavour; Thur–Tue 9am–7pm; charge; www.palazzo-medici.it). In 1439, Cosimo Il Vecchio, founder of the Medici dynasty, commissioned Brunelleschi's student Michelozzo to build the first home of the Medici clan, where they would live until 1540 when Cosimo I moved to the Palazzo Vecchio *(see page 33)* and then to the Palazzo Pitti *(see page 69)*; today it houses Florence's *carabinieri-* (police-) guarded Prefecture.

The palazzo's ground-floor museum is often used for special exhibits, but its real attraction is the renovated Cappella dei Magi on the first floor. It contains Benozzo Gozzoli's famous fresco, the *Procession of the Magi*, painted 1459–63, a lavish pictorial record in rich, warm colours of everybody who was anybody in 15th-century Florence, including the whole Medici clan and a self-portrait of the light-blue-hatted artist.

SAN MARCO

North of the city centre, facing onto Piazza San Marco, the Dominican church and monastery of **San Marco** (Mon–Sat 8.30am–noon, 4–6pm, Sun 4–6pm) houses one of Florence's most evocative museums: the **Museo di San Marco** (Mon–Fri 8.15am–1.50pm, Sat–Sun 8.15am–5pm, closed 1st, 3rd and 5th Sun of the month; charge; www.polomuseale.firenze.it). Florentine-born Fra Angelico (1387–1455) lived here as a monk, and most of his finest paintings and frescoes, including the great *Deposition* altarpiece, can be seen in the Pilgrim's Hospice *(Ospizio dei Pelligrini)*, to the right of the entrance. Follow signs to the small Refectory *(Refettorio)*, decorated with a vivid Ghirlandaio mural of *The Last Supper* (a favourite subject for monastery dining halls and one of seven in Florence).

The cloister bell resting placidly in the Sala della Capitolo has had a chequered career. Donated by Cosimo de' Medici, it was known as *La Piagnona* (The

San Marco faithful

Great Moaner); the puritanical supporters of Savonarola, at one time a prior here, were nicknamed *I Piagnoni* after it, and it was tolled to alert the monks when the friar's enemies came to arrest him in 1498 *(see page 21)*. For this act of treason, the bell was spitefully condemned to 50 years of exile outside the city, and was whipped through the streets all the way out of town.

Upstairs in the dormitory, you can visit the monks' cells, each one bearing a fresco by Fra Angelico or one of his pupils. His masterpiece, the famous *Annunciation*, is located at the top of the stairs, and another version can be found in cell number 3. At the end of the row to the right of the stairs are the two cells (38 and 39) once reserved for Cosimo de' Medici's meditations, and at the

Healing gardens

On the eastern side of San Marco is the delightful Giardino dei Semplici (Mon–Tue, Thur–Fri 9am–1pm, Sat 9am–5pm; charge). Now part of the university, the garden was begun by Duke Cosimo in 1545. Initially it was used to grow medicinal herbs, hence its name, but today tropical plants and Tuscan flora have been added to the collection.

farthest end of the dormitory are the quarters of Girolamo Savonarola *(see above and page 20)*, the monastery's fire-and-brimstone prior and sworn enemy of the Medici.

The architect Michelozzo expanded the 13th-century monastery in 1437. His superb colonnaded library leads off the dormitory and is now used for rotating exhibits.

Michelangelo's masterpiece

Galleria dell'Accademia

At the east end of Piazza San Marco is a 14th-century loggia and the entrance to the Accademia di Belle Arti (Fine Arts). Founded by Cosimo I in the 16th century, the school was enlarged in 1784 with an exhibition hall and a collection of Florentine paintings. The entrance to the **Galleria dell'Accademia** (Tue–Sun 8.15am–6.50pm; charge; www.polomuseale.firenze.it) is on Via Ricasoli, south of the loggia. It is a small but important collection of 13th–16th-century paintings, tapestries and furniture, including some typical Florentine marriage chests.

The gallery's main attraction is its seven sculptures by Michelangelo, whose stand-out centrepiece is the 4.5m (15ft) **David**, perhaps the most famous piece of sculpture in the Western world. Brought here from the Piazza della Signoria in 1873, it is displayed in a purpose-built domed room. Commissioned in 1501 as a symbol of Florence, upon its completion Michelangelo was just 26 years old. Its balanced and harmonious composition and mastery of technique instantly established it as a masterpiece. Recently cleaned, the marble has regained its original brightness, making the statue even more impressive.

The other works here are the four *Prisoners*, providing a remarkable illustration of Michelangelo's technique as they emerge from the rough stone. He claimed that all his sculptures already existed within the block of marble, and that he only had to release them. These figures, apparently struggling to break out of the rough marble which holds them as prisoners, offer a wonderful expression of his philosophy.

Also part of the Accademia, the displays in the **Museo degli Strumenti Musicali** (same times and ticket as for the Accademia) comprise instruments from the 17th–19th centuries. Among the most important pieces are a Stradivari violin, a cello by Amati and the world's oldest surviving upright piano.

Piazza della Santissima Annunziata

From the Piazza San Marco, a walk along Via C. Battisti leads to the **Piazza della Santissima Annunziata**, Florence's prettiest square and perhaps the finest example of Renaissance architecture (and proportion) in the city.

The piazza, with graceful colonnades on three sides, was probably designed by Brunelleschi when he built the square's

The *David*

The promising young Michelangelo had just completed the *Pietà* (now on display in Rome's St Peter's Basilica) when he was commissioned to do the *David* in 1501, the one masterwork most immediately associated with the master Florentine artist who will for ever be considered the Renaissance's most influential force. One detractor, the 19th-century Grand Tourist and essayist William Hazlitt, described it as 'an awkward overgrown actor at one of our minor theatres, without his clothes'. Those who come today to stand in quiet awe are more inclined to agree with D.H. Lawrence, who considered it 'the genius of Florence'. A life-size marble copy stands in front of the Palazzo Vecchio in the Piazza della Signoria, while a bronze replica anchors the hilltop Piazzale Michelangelo, where the magical sunset views over Florence are the same as those which influenced Florence's most famous son over 500 years ago.

Spedale degli Innocenti *(see below)* in the early 1440s. On the north side, the church of **Santissima Annunziata** (daily 7am–noon, 4–7pm) was completed in 1481. The architect, Michelozzo, conformed to Brunelleschi's original vision, ensuring the piazza's lasting harmony. The two 17th-century fountains by Tacca, and Giambologna's equestrian statue of Grand Duke Ferdinando I, add to the square's feeling of spaciousness.

The church entrance leads to an atrium decorated with frescoes by Andrea del Sarto and others, from which a door gives access to the extravagantly decorated interior. Immediately left of the entrance, the 15th-century shrine of the Annunziata shelters an old painting of the *Annunciation*, displayed only on special feast days and said to have been painted by a monk with the help of an angel. Reputed to have miraculous properties, it has been the object of pilgrimages and offerings for centuries.

The Foundling Hospital

The **Galleria dello Spedale degli Innocenti** (Mon–Sat 8.30am–7pm, Sun 8.30am–2pm; charge), on the east side of the square, exhibits 15th-

One of della Robbia's babies on the Spedale degli Innocenti

and 16th-century sculptures and paintings belonging to Florence's Foundling Hospital (*Spedale degli Innocenti* means 'Hospital of the Innocents'). Built to Brunelleschi's design in the 1440s, it was the first foundling hospital in Europe. Note the 15th-century glazed terracotta roundels of swaddled babes by Andrea della Robbia on the arched facade – these are the 'della Robbia babies' that so appealed to Lucy Honeychurch, the heroine of E.M. Forster's novel *A Room with a View*. Under the northern end of the colonnade is the small door where abandoned babies were left.

Museo Archeologico and Tempio Ebraico

The archway to the left/north of the Spedale leads out of the piazza and to the Via della Colonna and the **Museo Archeologico** (Mon 2–7pm, Wed and Thur 8.30am–7pm, Tue and Fri–Sun 8.30am–2pm; charge; www.firenze musei.it), housed in what was once the palace of a grand

The distinctive Tempio Ebraico

duke and boasting important collections of ancient Egyptian, Greek and Etruscan art, especially the collection of bronzes that includes the famous *Chimera* (5th century BC). The superbly reconstructed Etruscan tombs in the gardens were damaged in the 1966 flood but have since been restored.

Beyond the Archaeological Museum, just off Via della Colonna on Via Luigi Carlo Farini, is the **Tempio Ebraico** (Sun–Thur 10am–1pm, 2–4pm, Fri 10am–1pm; charge; www.moked.it/firenzebraica). Florence's huge Jewish synagogue is easily recognised by its green, copper-covered dome. It was built in the Hispano-Moroccan style between 1874 and 1882 on the site of the ghetto, founded by Cosimo I in 1551.

Cappellone degli Spagnoli's colourful interior

SANTA MARIA NOVELLA

The first view of Florence for travellers emerging from the railway station is the slender campanile of Santa Maria Novella rising across the square. This is only the back view of one of Florence's greatest monastic churches; to appreciate the beauty of its multicoloured marble facade you must walk around into **Piazza Santa Maria Novella**.

Santa Maria Novella

The cavernous church of **Santa Maria Novella** (Mon–Thur and Sat 9am–5pm, Fri and Sun 1–5pm, last entry 30 mins before closing; charge; www.smn.it) was designed by Dominican architects in the mid-13th century, and a small Dominican community still resides within its walls. The upper part of the bold, inlaid marble front was completed in 1470 in Renaissance style by the architect Leon Battista

Alberti, who was also responsible for the graceful Palazzo Rucellai nearby. (The lower Gothic facade is a century older.) One of the few Florentine churches the Medici didn't pay for, Santa Maria Novella was funded by the Rucellai family; they had their name put up in large Roman letters under the top cornice, and had the family emblem of a billowing sail repeated along the frieze to make sure their generosity wouldn't go unnoticed.

Walk beneath the soaring vaults of the 100m (328ft) tall nave to the cluster of richly frescoed family chapels surrounding the altar. The chancel is decorated with a dazzling fresco cycle by Ghirlandaio depicting *Scenes from the Lives of the Virgin and St John*, which were paid for by the wealthy Tornabuoni family. Ghirlandaio, Florence's leading 'social' painter of the late 15th century, peopled his biblical frescoes with members of the Tornabuoni clan – one of whom was the mother of Lorenzo Il Magnifico – all dressed in the latest everyday fashions.

To the right of the altar is the **Filippo Strozzi Chapel**, colourfully frescoed by Filippino Lippi, son of the painter Fra Filippo, and the **Bardi Chapel**, with 14th-century frescoes. **The Gondi Chapel** to the left of the altar contains a Brunelleschi crucifix (his reply to Donatello's

Turtle tracks

Before leaving Piazza Santa Maria Novella, note the stone obelisks supported by Giambologna's bronze turtles. They marked the boundaries of horse races and chicken races common from approximately 1550 to 1850.

'peasant' crucifix in Santa Croce; *see page 47*); it is his only work in wood. On the extreme left is the **Strozzi Chapel**, with 14th-century frescoes of *The Last Judgement, Heaven* and *Hell* – its benefactors, of course, are depicted in Heaven.

The church's most striking work is Masaccio's *Trinity* (c.1427) on the wall of the left aisle. Famous for the first such handling of early perspective and a convincing illusion of depth, the fresco depicts the crucifixion in a purely Renaissance architectural setting, dramatically breaking from the established canons of religious art.

The Cloister and Spanish Chapel

To the left of the church lies what remains of the monastery, part of which has been taken over by the *carabinieri* and is closed to the public. Exit the church for the separate entrance to the great 14th-century cloister with its three giant cypresses. Known as the **Chiostro Verde** (Green Cloister) after the greenish tint of the frescoes of the *Universal Deluge* by Paolo Uccello, it is flanked by the Refectory (where some detached surviving frescoes are now preserved); a smaller cloister; and the famous **Cappellone degli Spagnoli** (Spanish Chapel), an impressive, vaulted chapter-house named in honour of Cosimo I's Spanish wife, Eleonora of Toledo. Gigantic 14th-century frescoes by the little-known Andrea da Firenze cover its four walls. The artist incorporated a picture of the Duomo complete with its cupola – 60 years before it was actually completed.

Cascine Park

A 15-minute walk west along the river from Ognissanti will bring you to Le Cascine, a pleasant park that runs along the embankment west of the city for 3km (2 miles). Cascina means 'dairy farm', and that is what it was until it was acquired by Duke Alessandro de' Medici and laid out as a park by his successor, Cosimo I.

Museo Marino Marini

South of Piazza Santa Maria Novella, the Via dei Fossi – lined with antiques shops – leads down to the riverside **Piazza Goldoni**. A little way down Via dei Fossi, on the left Via della Spada leads to the **Museo Marino Marini** (Mon and Wed–Fri 10am–5pm; charge; www.museo marinomarini.it). Set in the old San Pancrazio church, the museum has an excellent collection of the 20th-century sculptor's work.

Ognissanti

From Piazza Goldoni, Borgo Ognissanti leads towards the church of **Ognissanti** (All Saints; Sat–Thur 7.15am–

Storm clouds gather over Ognissanti

12.30pm). Contrary to the impression given by its fine 17th-century facade and the della Robbia glazed-terracotta relief over the doorway, the church dates from around 1250. Its builders, the *Umiliati* ('Humble Ones'), were a monastic community who, ironically, ran a remarkably lucrative wool business and were among the first to put Florence on the road to financial prosperity. The church contains Botticelli's *St Augustine*, and in the Refectory, Ghirlandaio's other famous *Last Supper (Cenacolo)*, both commissioned by the wealthy Vespucci family (famous for the navigator and cartographer, Amerigo, who lent his name to the New World), several of whose members are buried here, as is Botticelli himself.

The Ponte Vecchio reflected in the Arno

THE OLTRARNO

The district on the south bank of the river, called the Oltrarno ('beyond the Arno'), contains some of Florence's most characterful neighbourhoods.

Ponte Vecchio

The oldest bridge in Florence, the **Ponte Vecchio** was the only one spared destruction in World War II (though both sides of its banks were bombed; notice how the buildings date from the 1950s). The present bridge, lined with jewellers' and goldsmiths' workshops overhanging the river, dates back to 1345. From the terrace in the middle of the bridge, you can look west towards the softly curved arches of the elegant **Ponte Santa Trinità**. One of the many blown up by the retreating Germans in August 1944, this bridge was carefully reconstructed, exactly as Ammannati had built it in the 16th century.

Via de' Guicciardini passes the church of **Santa Felicità** (Mon–Sat 9.30am–noon, 3.30–5.30pm) on the way towards Piazza de' Pitti. Inside are two works by the Mannerist artist Pontormo (1494–1557), an *Annunciation* and a *Deposition*.

Palazzo Pitti

On Piazza de' Pitti is the huge **Palazzo Pitti**. This palace was built as a symbol of wealth and power by the Florentine merchant Luca Pitti, who wanted to impress his rivals, the Medici. Begun in 1457, it was continuously enlarged until the 19th century. Pitti died (together with his savings) in 1472, but the Medici were sufficiently impressed by his palace to buy it in 1549, enlarging it substantially, after which it served as the official residence of the Medici (beginning with Cosimo I and his wife Eleonora of Toledo) and the successive ruling families of Florence until 1919, when it was bequeathed to the country. The palace and grounds contain five museums and galleries.

Palatine Gallery and Royal Apartments

The sumptuous **Galleria Palatina** and the **Appartamenti Reali** (Palatine Gallery and Royal Apartments; Tue–Sun 8.15am–6.50pm; charge; www.polomuseale.firenze.it) are the main attraction of the Palazzo Pitti complex. The latter, whose name is misleading as the inhabiting families were not monarchs, consists of 14 lavishly decorated rooms. The former preserves the magnificent art collection of the Medici and Lorraine grand dukes, just as the owners hung them – a jigsaw puzzle according to theme and personal preference rather than historical sequence. Priceless paintings decorate 26 dazzling rooms, hung four-high amid gilded, stuccoed and frescoed decoration. It is the largest and most important collection of paintings in Florence after the Uffizi. There are superb works by masters such as Titian, Rubens, Raphael, Botticelli, Velázquez and Murillo, exhibited in grandiose halls

Part of the impressive
Palazzo Pitti

adorned with ceiling paintings of classical themes, such as the Hall of the Iliad and the Hall of Venus.

The Modern Art, Costume and Silver Museums

The best of 19th- and 20th-century Italian art can be seen in the interesting **Galleria d'Arte Moderna** (Gallery of Modern Art; Tue–Sun 8.15am–6.50pm; charge), on the floor above the Palatina. Here you can discover the exciting works of Tuscany's own Impressionist movement, the *Macchiaioli* (or 'spot-painters') of the 1860s. In 1999, 100 new paintings were added to the already fascinating collection.

Also inside the palace is the **Galleria del Costume**. The museum showcases fashions from the 18th century to the present day (daily Nov–Feb 8.15am–4.30pm, Mar and Oct 8.15am–5.30pm, Apr–May and Sept 8.15am–6.30pm, June–Aug 8.15am–6.50pm; charge).

Sixteen sumptuous rooms comprise the **Museo degli Argenti** (Silverware Museum; same times and charge as the Galleria del Costume), with some of the Medici's most cherished jewellery, gold, silver, cameos, crystal, ivory, furniture and porcelain, including Lorenzo Il Magnifico's priceless collection of 16 exquisite antique vases. The room in which they are displayed is the biggest surprise of all, with 17th-century frescoes that create a dizzying optical illusion of extra height and depth.

The Garden and the Porcelain Museum

Once you've seen the galleries, take a relaxing stroll in the delightful **Giardino di Boboli** (daily Nov–Feb 8.15am–4.30pm, Mar and Oct until 5.30pm, Apr–May and Sept until 6.30pm, June–Aug until 7.30pm, last entry 1 hour before closing; entrance included in ticket for Costume, Silverware and Porcelain museums), an Italian pleasure-garden of arbours and cypress-lined avenues dotted with graceful statuary, lodges, grottoes and fountains. The entrance to the gardens, at the back of the palace courtyard, leads to the amphitheatre, which has a fine view of the palace and the city beyond.

Up the hill behind it are the Vasca del Nettuno (Neptune Fountain) and the Palazzina detta 'del Cavaliere', housing the **Museo delle Porcellane** (same times and charge as the Galleria del Costume), a fine porcelain collection. Off to the right, at the end of a long cypress avenue, is the Piazzale dell'Isolotto, an idyllic island of greenery, fountains and sculpture set in an ornamental pond.

Returning downhill, head right just below the amphitheatre to see the **Grotta di Buontalenti** (guided tours only, daily Apr–Sept 11am, 1pm, 3pm, 4pm and 5pm, Oct–Mar 11am, 1pm and 3pm), a fake grotto full of sculptures, as well as the much-photographed statue of Cosimo I's court jester, a pot-bellied dwarf, riding on the back of a turtle.

Checking out the view from the Museo delle Porcellane

Santo Spirito

Turning left out of the Palazzo Pitti, walking up to the nearby Piazza San Felice and then right along Via Mazzetta brings you to the attractive, tree-lined **Piazza Santo Spirito**, with its morning market stalls and pavement cafés. The modest pale-golden facade rising above the back of the piazza is the church of **Santo Spirito** (Mon–Tue and Thur–Sat 9.30am–12.30pm, 4–5.30pm, Wed 10am–noon, Sun 11.30am–noon). A monastic foundation of the Augustinian order dating back to the 13th century, the present church was designed by Brunelleschi and built in the second half of the 15th century. The bare, unfinished exterior conceals a masterpiece of Renaissance architectural harmony. The interior's walls are lined with 39 elegant side altars, while slender, grey, stone columns with Corinthian capitals, along with an interplay of arches and vaulted aisles, create an impression of tremendous space.

Santa Maria del Carmine

Further west, the unpretentious church of **Santa Maria del Carmine** (Mon–Sat 9am–noon, 5–5.30pm, Sun 9–10am, 11am–noon, 5–5.30pm) houses some of the seminal frescoes of the Renaissance. A young Masaccio and his teacher Masolino, commissioned by the wealthy merchant Felice Brancacci, worked from 1425 to 1427 on the decorations for the **Cappella Brancacci** (Mon and Wed–Sat 10am–5pm, Sun 1–5pm; charge) at the end of the right transept. Masolino's own work is striking enough, but Masaccio's *The Tribute Money* and *The Expulsion of Adam and Eve from the Garden of Eden*

Artistic pilgrimage

It is said that Florentine artists young and old made pilgrimages to the Brancacci Chapel to marvel at and learn from Masaccio's achievement (stories recount visits by Michelangelo and Leonardo, who sat and sketched).

raised the art of painting to what was an unprecedented level. His feeling for light and space, his dramatic stage-set figures, and the solidity of their forms were considered little short of an inspired miracle. Nothing like them had been painted before; the Renaissance had truly arrived. Sadly, Masaccio died at the age of 27, in 1428.

A devastating fire in 1771 somehow left the Brancacci frescoes intact, but elsewhere in the church you will see the late Baroque architecture and styling used to recreate the church. Opposite the Brancacci Chapel is the Corsini Chapel, a rare jewel of the Florentine Baroque style.

Masaccio's *Adam and Eve* in the Brancacci Chapel

Piazzale Michelangelo and San Miniato al Monte

Back at the Ponte Vecchio, the Via dei Bardi leads east to the Piazza Santa Maria Soprarno. A little farther along is the lovely small **Museo Bardini** (currently closed for restoration; www.polomuseale.firenze.it). Housed in a building constructed from bits of ancient buildings that were being demolished, this eclectic art collection was left to the city by the antiques dealer Stefano Bardini in 1923. Particularly impressive are the Andrea della Robbia tomb, a *Madonna* that is attributed to Donatello, Pollaiuolo's *St Michael* and a headless *Virgin* (c.1300) by Giovanni Pisano.

Continuing east along Via di San Niccolò, a right turn up Via San Miniato will bring you to Porta San Miniato, one of the few surviving gateways from the 14th-century city wall. On the other side of the wall, follow Via dei Bastoni parallel with the wall until you reach a set of stone steps on the right that leads straight uphill, passing through leafy gardens and interrupted occasionally by a switchback road. At the top of the series of steps is the **Piazzale Michelangelo**. If you cannot manage or face the climb, buses 12 and 13 run here from Ponte alle Grazie. The square was laid out in the 19th century and is dotted with reproductions of Michelangelo's sculptures, not to mention scores of tour buses and souvenir stalls. The views are absolutely marvellous; it is from here that all those classic postcard pictures of the rooftops of Florence are taken.

The church of **San Miniato al Monte** (daily Apr–Oct 8am–7pm, Nov–Mar 8am–1pm, 2.30–6pm), arguably the most beautiful in Florence and beloved by Florentines, enjoys a magnificent hilltop location above Piazzale Michelangelo. St Minias, an early Christian martyred during the 3rd century AD, is said to have carried his own severed head up to this hilltop and set it down on the spot where the church was later built. Rebuilt in the early 11th century, it is a remarkable example of Florentine-style Romanesque architecture. The superb green-and-white marble facade, visible from Florence below, contains a 13th-century mosaic representing Christ flanked by St Minias and the Virgin Mary. The cool, mystical interior has all the splendour of a Byzantine basilica, with its wealth of richly inlaid marble and mosaic decorations. Note the painted wooden ceiling, and the nave's 13th-century oriental-carpet-like marble pavement.

Beside the church, the **Cimetero Monumentale delle Porte Sante** dates back to 1864, when burials in the historic centre of Florence were banned. Look for the tomb of Tuscan-born Carlo Collodi (born Lorenzini), the author of *Pinocchio*.

A chance to escape the heat of the city

EXCURSIONS

Within easy reach of a day trip from Florence are some of Tuscany's most impressive attractions. On the hills above the city is the village of Fiesole, and in the neighbouring Chianti district the spectacular towers of San Gimignano. A little farther afield are the cities of Pisa and Siena, the latter a great rival to Florence, crammed with artworks and beautiful architecture.

Fiesole

A winding road climbs for some 8km (5 miles) through the outlying neighbourhoods north of Florence to the charming little hilltop town of **Fiesole** (take the No. 7 bus from Santa Maria Novella railway station or Piazza San Marco). An ancient Etruscan stronghold and later a Roman settlement, it provides an escape from the city's summer heat, and offers wonderful views over Florence and the Arno Valley.

Superb views of Fiesole from the Via di San Francesco

Piazza Mino

The bus drops you in the central **Piazza Mino**, which has a market on Saturdays and a couple of pleasant cafés. Opposite the bus stop is Fiesole's cathedral. Founded in 1028 and completed during the 13th and 14th centuries, **San Romolo** (daily Apr–Oct 7.30am–noon, 3–7pm, Nov–Mar 7.30am–noon, 3–5pm) was totally restored in the 19th century, leaving it with a rather drab exterior. Its campanile, visible for miles around, dates back to 1213. A Byzantine atmosphere pervades the interior, which contains the Capella Salutati, with two works by Mino da Fiesole – a tabernacle showing the *Virgin with Saints*, and the tomb of Bishop Salutati.

To the right of the cathedral is the arched entrance to the **Roman Theatre** and its adjacent archaeological site, the **Zona Archeologica** (Apr–Sept daily 9.30am–7pm, Nov–Mar Thur–Mon 9.30am–5pm; charge). The well-preserved theatre dates from around 100BC and seats some 2,500 spectators. Half original and half restored, it is still sometimes used for performances. Below the theatre are the remains of Roman baths and a temple. A small but interesting archaeological museum is housed in a replica of the temple inside the entrance. Just opposite the site is the **Museo Bandini** (same times and ticket as the Roman Theatre), with a collection of paintings by the so-called Italian Primitives.

From the square, follow the signs for the extremely steep but picturesque **Via di San Francesco** uphill to the church of **San Francesco** (Mon–Sat 9.30am–noon, 3–6pm, Sun 3–6pm) and its tiny monastery. The views of Florence from the terrace below the church are gorgeous, and the monastery (and its quirky, free museum of antiquities), with its peaceful little cloisters, is enchanting. A wooded park offers a choice of footpaths back down the hill.

Between Fiesole and Florence

From the southwest corner of the Piazza Mino, the steep **Via Vecchia Fiesolana**, the original road to the town, zigzags down the hillside towards Florence. Over the centuries various villas have been built here to take advantage of the breathtaking views, including **Villa Medici,** built here in 1458–61 by Michelozzo for Cosimo de' Medici.

You rejoin the main road at the 15th-century Dominican church and monastery of **San Domenico** (daily 9am–2pm, 5–8pm). This is where Fra Angelico took his vows; his fine fresco of *The Crucifixion* adorns the Chapterhouse.

Just before the church, a right turn leads to the **Badia Fiesolana** (Mon–Fri 9am–5pm, Sat 9am–noon), which was Fiesole's cathedral until 1028. Rebuilt by Cosimo Il Vecchio in the 15th century, it is a gem of Renaissance architecture.

From San Domenico it is possible to catch the the No. 7 bus or enjoy the pleasant 4km (2½-mile) walk downhill through the Mugnone Valley and back to central Florence.

Pisa

Roughly 80km (50 miles) west of Florence lies Pisa, the birth-place of Galileo, and home of the fabled Leaning Tower. The city was a flourishing commercial centre and port during the Middle Ages, until the silting-up of the Arno estuary left it stranded – 11km (7 miles) inland from the coast. The most conspicuous legacy of Pisa's wealthy and powerful past, and what everybody comes to admire, are the architectural wonders of the **Campo dei Miracoli** (Field of Miracles, or Piaz-za del Duomo) – the Duomo, the Battistero and, of course, the cathedral's circular campanile, the Leaning Tower.

The centrepiece of the Field of Miracles is the white marble **Duomo** (Nov–Feb daily 10am–1pm, 2–5pm, Mar and Oct daily 10am–7pm, Apr–Sept Mon–Sat 10am–8pm, Sun 1–8pm; charge; www.opapisa.it). It is the most important and influ-ential Romanesque building in Tuscany, and the first to use the much-copied horizontal 'banding' of grey-and-white mar-ble stripes. It was begun *c*.1063 and completed by the 13th century (its bronze doors facing the tower date from 1180). The striped decoration is repeated in the vast interior, which also boasts an ornate wooden ceiling. The cathedral's master-piece, however, is the magnificent carved pulpit by the local Giovanni Pisano (1302–10). Opposite the pulpit is the 16th-century **Galileo Lamp**, whose workings inspired his theory of pendulum movement. The apse's dazzling mosaics depicting **Christ Pantocrator** were finished in 1302 by Cimabue.

The **Battistero** (Baptistery; daily Nov–Feb 10am–5pm, Mar 9am–6pm, Apr–Sept 8am–8pm, Oct 9am–7pm; charge), was started in 1152 but not completed until the 14th cen-tury. The sparsely decorated interior, famous for its excellent acoustics, contains a superb hexagonal pulpit carved in 1260 by Nicola Pisano, father of Andrea and Giovanni.

However, it is the world-famous, 57m (187ft) campanile of the cathedral, the **Torre Pendente** (Leaning Tower; daily

Nov–Feb 10am–5pm, Mar and Oct 9am–6pm, Apr–Sept 8.30am–8.30pm; charge; www.opapisa.it), which really captures the eye, just as beautiful and delicate as carved ivory, and now leaning out of true verticality by 4.5m (15ft), though measurements vary. Begun after the Duomo and Baptistery in 1173, it began to lean when only three of the eight storeys had been completed, since the shifting ground beneath the Campo is waterlogged sand – hardly ideal foundation material (the Duomo and Baptistery are also marginally off kilter). Various architects attempted to correct the lean as con-

Pisa's most famous sight

struction work continued, resulting in a slight bend by the time of the tower's completion in 1372. A remarkable engineering project has saved the tower from collapse.

On the north side of the piazza is the walled **Camposanto**, a unique 13th-century, cloister-like cemetery (filled with sacred soil brought back from the Holy Land; daily Mar and Oct 9am–6pm, Apr–Sept 8am–8pm; charge), the walls of which were once covered with remarkable 14th–15th-century frescoes, some by Benozzo Gozzoli. These were badly damaged during World War II bombing raids, and were removed to the **Museo delle Sinopie** (daily Mar and Oct 9am–6pm, Apr–Sept 8am–8pm; charge) in Piazza del Duomo. The **Museo del Duomo** (daily Mar and Oct 9am–6pm, Apr–Sept 8am–

8pm; charge), housed in a former 13th-century monastery in the Piazza del Duomo, shelters a wealth of artwork taken from the Duomo and Baptistery.

Siena

Siena, around 34km (21 miles) south of Florence, is still a medieval hilltop city. Its walls enclose a maze of narrow, winding streets that have survived virtually unchanged since the 16th century and earlier. As you approach Siena along a road cut through a succession of undulating hills covered with a rich, reddish-brown soil, you'll understand how the colour 'burnt sienna' came by its name.

The city itself is a wonderful marriage of brick and stone, all weathered reds and warm pinks. Imposing Gothic architecture prevails within the city walls, from the main square's early 14th-century Palazzo Pubblico, with its graceful and slender 97m (320ft) tower, the Torre del Mangia, to the grand zebra-striped cathedral and many fine palazzos.

Siena's Palio

If you're in Italy on 2 July or 16 August, it's worth going out of your way to see the Palio, a traditional bareback horse race held in the Piazza del Campo since the 13th century. Try to reserve a seat in the stands or a place on a balcony with a view, as the Campo (where no tickets are needed for the huge, emotional crowd in the summer heat) can be, at best, uncomfortable. After a stately hour-long parade of colourful pages, men-at-arms, knights and flag-twirlers dressed in 15th-century costumes, 10 fiercely competitive bareback riders, each representing a different *contrada* (city ward), battle it out during three wild laps around the dirt-covered piazza. The winning *contrada* is awarded the coveted Palio, a painted silken standard. The only rule is that the riders must not interfere with each other's reins; otherwise, anything goes – and often does.

Piazza del Campo

The heart of the city is the huge, sloping, fan-shaped **Piazza del Campo** (commonly known as Il Campo), where the Palio horse race *(see box opposite)* takes place twice each summer, with tickets virtually impossible to obtain. Siena's atmosphere of aristocratic grandeur befits the proud Ghibelline stronghold it once was. According to ancient myth, it was founded

The view over Piazza del Campo from the Torre del Mangia

by the descendants of Remus (whose twin brother Romulus founded Rome), while in reality it was colonised by the ancient Romans under Augustus. This most stubbornly independent of Tuscan cities fell under Florentine sway until 1555 and, soon thereafter, slipped into a centuries-long slumber.

Within the Campo's **Palazzo Pubblico** is the **Museo Civico** (daily Mar–Oct 10am–7pm, Nov–Feb 10am–6pm; charge; www.comune.siena.it), where you can see Siena-born artist Simone Martini's early yet important frescoes of the *Maestà* (Madonna Enthroned; 1315), and the *Condottiere Guidoriccio da Fogliano* (1328) on his richly caparisoned horse. In the next room are local master Ambrogio Lorenzetti's impressive allegorical frescoes, *The Effect of Good and Bad Government* (1339), one of the largest medieval paintings of a secular theme.

Piazza del Duomo

Almost all of historic Siena is closed to traffic. Wander freely through the picturesque, winding and hilly streets to the great Gothic **Duomo** (June–Aug Mon–Sat 10.30am–8pm, Sun 1.30–6.30pm, Mar–May and Sept–Oct Mon–Sat 10.30am–

7.30pm, Sun 1.30–5.30pm, Nov–Feb Mon–Sat 10.30am–6.30pm, Sun 1.30–5.30pm; charge; www.operaduomo.siena.it). Perched atop Siena's highest point and begun in 1196, it's visible from afar for its striking black-and-white striped exterior – a motif repeated in the city's coat of arms. The attractions within include the uniquely intricate inlaid marble floor, a splendid sculptured octagonal pulpit (1265) by Nicola Pisano, and Pinturicchio's colourful historical frescoes (1509) in the adjoining Piccolomini Library.

In the neighbouring **Museo dell'Opera del Duomo** (daily Mar–May and Sept–Nov 9.30am–7pm, June–Aug 9.30am–8pm, Nov–Feb 10am–5pm; charge; www.operaduomo.siena.it), the splendid *Maestà* (1308) by local master painter Duccio is the focal point. He is one of the leading Italian painters of Siena's important 13th- and 14th-century school of art, whose finest examples are on display in the city's art gallery, the **Pinacoteca Nazionale** (Tue–Sat 10am–5.15pm, Mon 8.30am–1.30pm; charge), housed south of the Duomo in the imposing Palazzo Buonsignori.

San Gimignano

The walled medieval town of San Gimignano is one of Italy's most evocative. Strategically set on a hilltop, its skyline bristles with the angular outlines of traditional 12th–13th-century Tuscan tower-houses. At one time the town boasted over 70 – it was a matter of prestige to build the tallest tower possible. Today, just over a dozen remain, but that's more than enough to make it the best-preserved (and most popular) medieval town in Tuscany, and to earn it the proud name '*delle belle torri*' (of the beautiful towers) and the crowds of tourists that go with it.

Here you can stroll through streets and squares barely changed since Dante arrived as a Florentine envoy in 1300. The plain-facaded 12th-century **Collegiata** church (also called the Duomo, though it is not officially a cathedral; Mar and Nov–Jan Mon–Sat 9.30am–4.40pm, Sun 12.30–4.40pm; Apr–Oct Mon–Fri 9.30am–7.10pm, Sat 9.30am–5.10pm, Sun 12.30–5.10pm; charge) is filled with impressive frescoes. Its tiny **Cappella di Santa Fina** (1475) is decorated with elegant Ghirlandaio murals depicting San Gimignano's towers in the background. Santa Fina, only 15 years old when she died in 1253, was a local mystic who was adopted as one of the town's patron saints (together with San Gimignano himself).

The 13th–14th-century **Palazzo del Popolo** (Town Hall), with its 36m (117ft) tower, contains the **Museo Civico** and **Pinacoteca** (daily Mar–Oct 9.30am–7pm, Nov–Feb 10am–5pm; charge). The **Torre Grossa** has a superb little courtyard, and unusual frescoes of hunting and courtly love. At the highest point in town is the **Rocca** (Citadel), offering superb panoramic views.

Medieval San Gimignano, the town of towers

Be sure to visit the 13th-century church of **Sant'Agostino** for its fresco cycle (in the choir) by 15th-century Florentine painter Gozzoli, depicting *Scenes from the Life of St Augustine*. Also worth a visit is the **Museo Archeologico** (Nov–Dec Sat–Thur 11am–6pm; Apr–Oct daily 11am–6pm, charge; www.archeologiatoscana.it), on Via Folgore.

WHAT TO DO

SHOPPING

Since the Middle Ages, Florentines have held craftsmanship in high regard, and the city's elegant shops are famed for the quality of their merchandise, especially jewellery (particularly gold), leather goods, antiques and fashion. It is one of Italy's best shopping destinations and one that promises good window-shopping.

Beautifully dressed shop windows compete for your attention along expensive Via dei Tornabuoni, location of Gucci, Tod's, Ferragamo and Roberto Cavalli. The Florentine house Pucci can be found on Via de' Pucci. Other good hunting grounds are the slightly less chic Via de' Calzaiuoli and Via Roma and their offshoots.

Tourist and souvenir **markets** *(see page 90)* are held daily in the sprawling San Lorenzo area, and the less expansive Mercato Nuovo; a local market every Tuesday morning in the Cascine Park is less about souvenir-buying, but offers a colourful insight into Florentine life.

Most shops close for a period of 7–10 days (minimum) on and around 15 August. Some touristy shops in the centre of Florence choose not to close for the summer break. Most shops are open on Saturday afternoon; only a few open on Sunday; some are closed on Monday mornings.

Antiques and Reproductions

Antiques shops are clustered around the **Borgognissanti, Via della Vigna Nuova, Via dei Fossi** (and its parallel street Via del Moro) and **Via della Spada**, all on the north (Duomo) side of

Brightly coloured designs characterise Florentine brand Pucci

Glamorous shop window

the river; and in **Via Maggio** and **Via Santo Spirito** on the opposite bank in the Oltrarno neighbourhood. Specialising largely in furniture, paintings and decorations, none of them is inexpensive.

Bric-a-brac addicts will find a permanent, modest-sized flea market on **Piazza dei Ciompi** (the market is open daily in high season), with an overspill of shops in the area just behind the market. There is also an interesting antiques market the third full weekend of every month in the fountain park in front of the **Fortezza di Basso** along Viale degli Strozzi.

Framed 18th-century prints of Florence are good buys, especially in the shops around **Piazza del Duomo**. You can also look for unframed prints in the **San Lorenzo market**.

Ceramics

Regional ceramic specialities include expensive, high-quality table china (the well-known Richard Ginori china originated in Florence and is still produced outside of town), and brightly hand-painted ceramics of centuries-old Tuscan patterns and colours. Several great houseware stores in the centre carry selections of these goods at reasonable prices.

Gold and Silver

Designer gold jewellery is expensive (and almost always 18-carat), but simpler items such as gold (and occasionally silver) charms, chains and earrings are reasonably priced and widely available. Every piece should be stamped, confirming that it is solid gold (ask to see the stamp, as minuscule as it may be). The ultimate place to window-shop is, of course, along the **Ponte Vecchio**, a bridge lined with dazzling, centuries-old jewellers' shops, each window more tempting (and densely stocked) than the last.

The work of Florence's unsung silversmiths is invariably beautiful and practical. Look for pill boxes, napkin rings, photo frames, cruet sets, sugar bowls and candlesticks.

Inlays and Mosaics

The Florentine speciality of *intarsio*, the art of wood or semiprecious stone inlay, was perfected during the Renaissance (some examples can be seen in the Uffizi). The craft still flourishes, and you'll see modern interpretations (and replicas of classic patterns) for sale in **Lungarno Torrigiani, Via**

Antiques for sale on Via Maggio in Oltrarno

Guicciardini and **Piazza Santa Croce**. Larger items such as table tops are inevitably expensive and exorbitant to ship; small, framed 'naïve' pictures of birds, flowers, Tuscan landscapes or views of Florence are much less expensive.

Special papers

Florence has been a major centre of hand-printing and bookbinding for centuries, and these crafts have been resuscitated in the past few decades. Shops sell specialised stationery and items such as notebooks, frames and albums covered in handmade marbled paper. Leather-bound books such as diaries, address books and journals are beautifully crafted.

Leather

Florence has been known for its quality leather goods since the Middle Ages. This is the home town of the shoe- and bag-making greats Ferragamo and Gucci; the leather items for Prada and Fendi (associated, respectively, with Milan and Rome) are also produced in the Florentine foothills, demonstrating the city's dominance in this area. San Lorenzo's famous market is awash with good-value leather stalls (and the shops hidden behind them) that sell everything from handbags and luggage to wallets and gloves. Shoe shops are traditionally concentrated along **Via dei Calzaiuoli** ('The Street of Cobblers') and Borgo San Lorenzo.

The best buys in town are small leather goods: gloves, belts, purses, wallets and boxes, in all shapes and sizes and of varying quality. Handbags and outerwear can be gorgeous and tempting but are always expensive; less expensive variations can be found, in stores or the **San Lorenzo market**, but do not expect to get top-quality goods for knock-down prices: you get what you pay for.

Perfumes

Florence is home to one of the world's oldest apothecaries. The **Officina Profumo-Farmaceutica di Santa Maria Novella** (Via della Scala 16) was founded back in the 14th century by Dominican monks who used the premises to make herbal medicines. It was when they turned to making perfumes, and attracted the patronage of Catherine de' Medici, that their future success was assured. Today they still produce a wide range of traditional soaps and colognes (as well as a few innovations to keep up with the times), beautifully packaged and sold out of their shop – within an old 14th-century chapel – with its beautiful wooden and painted interior.

Florentine leather is famous for its quality

Street Markets

The biggest and most popular market is **San Lorenzo**, which caters to both tourists and locals, and sells everything from football banners to sunglasses, with an ever-growing emphasis on tourist-attracting goods. You'll find clothing (T-shirts, knitwear and woollen scarves), shoes and leatherwear, often at reasonable prices, but don't expect high-quality goods. Many stalls accept credit cards and travellers' cheques.

At its centre, stretching along Via dell' Ariento, is the late 19th-century structure that houses the **Mercato Centrale**, the city's largest and most colourful food market, bulging at the seams with just about everything from the surrounding Tuscan hills, from fresh fruit and vegetables to meat, fish and game. It is a great place for local colour, photo opportunities, insight into the Florentines' daily life and culinary heritage.

Shopping for groceries in the Mercato Centrale

The **Mercato Nuovo**, or **Straw Market**, is conveniently located halfway between the Duomo and the Ponte Vecchio. Housed beneath a 16th-century loggia, a score of stalls sell leather bags and other miscellaneous souvenirs – a far less expansive (and less interesting) selection than its big-sister market at San Lorenzo.

A daily **flea market** operates in Piazza dei Ciompi, selling the usual mix of junk and bric-a-brac found in flea markets the world over. A more genuine antiques market is also held in the same spot, and takes place on the last Sunday of each month.

San Ambrogio morning market in Piazza Ghiberti sells fresh foodstuffs, including pasta, porcini mushrooms and other Italian specialities.

A huge weekly market every Tuesday morning in **Cascine Park** sells all kinds of goods for a far less touristy clientele (little English is spoken). It's especially good for cheap clothes and shoes, as well as live chickens whose days are numbered.

ENTERTAINMENT

There's always something interesting going on in Florence. Information on current events can be found on the weekly 'what's on' posters throughout the city, and in the useful monthly publication *Firenze Spettacolo*, available from the tourist office. There are also weekly entertainment listings in the weekend edition of the Italian-language *La Repubblica*. It is cheapest, and very easy, to buy tickets directly from the venues where the concert or opera is taking place. The main venues are: Teatro Comunale, Corso Italia 16, tel: (055) 211 158, www.maggiofiorentino.com; Teatro Verdi, Via Ghibellina 99, tel: (055) 212 320, www.teatroverdifirenze.it; or Teatro della Pergola, Via della Pergola, tel: (055) 22641, www.pergola.firenze.it.

Music and Theatre

Summertime alfresco concerts are held in the **Boboli Garden**, and organ recitals are presented in historic churches in September and October (sporadically in winter months; remember there's no heating in these churches). During June, July and August, nearby **Fiesole** *(see pages 75–7)* offers the Estate Fiesolana festival of concerts, ballet, drama and film staged at the restored Roman amphitheatre, www.estate fiesolana.it. The opera season gets under way in December and runs until April, held mostly at the Teatro Comunale. An impressive chamber-music season is run by the **Amici della Musica** (www.amicimusica.fi.it) in the Teatro della Pergola.

The *centro storico* by night

Nightlife and Cinema

Florence's nightlife scene is fairly lively, and there are some good places to go for an *aperitivo* or cocktail. Of the currently fashionable, and more attractive, bars in the centre, try the **Dolce Vita** on Piazza del Carmine (www.dolcevitaflorence.com), the **Moyo** at Via dei Benci 23r (www.moyo.it) or **Il Rifrullo** at Via San Niccolò 55r (www.ilrifrullo.com). If you are looking for a club, of the few in or near the city centre worth a visit, two of the best are **YAB** (Via Sasseti 5r; www.yab.it) and **Central Park** (Via Fosso Macinate 1, Parco delle Cascine).

Most films screened in Florence are dubbed into Italian. The main venue for screening films in English is the Odeon Cinehall (www.cinehall.it) in Piazza Strozzi, which shows original-language films on Mondays, Tuesdays and Thursdays. During the summer, a fun, and cooler, way to see a film is at one of the outdoor cinemas located along the Viale or on the hillsides.

The Maggio

The highlight of the musical year in Florence is the Maggio Musicale (www.maggiofiorentino.com), from mid-May to the end of June, one of Italy's principal music festivals. It attracts some of the finest concert, ballet and operatic performers in the world, thanks in large part to the artistic direction of conductor Zubin Mehta.

SPORTS

Cycling. A national sport, as well as a great way to get around town. There are delightful rides in the surrounding countryside, too. Bikes are easy to hire *(see page 108)*.

Football. If cycling is a national sport then football *(calcio)* is a national passion. The local team is Fiorentina (http://it.violachannel.tv). They play in Serie A at the Stadio Artemio Franchi near the Campo di Marte railway station. If you are in Florence on or around the feast of St John (late June), you may want to catch the Calcio in Costume, where a rough-and-tumble medieval version of the game is played in period costume.

Walking. There are endless options for great walks in the rolling green hills that surround the city, in areas around Bellosguardo, Fiesole, the Certosa del Galluzzo monastery, Poggio Imperiale or the Arcetri observatory (which stands on the hill from which Galileo gazed at the stars), all within easy reach of Florence, but where you'll feel like you're out in the beautiful countryside of Tuscany. The tourist office can supply useful walking maps of the province.

CHILDREN'S FLORENCE

Young children quickly tire of visiting museums and galleries, especially in the heat of summer. To keep things running smoothly, intersperse museum visits with ice cream from the city's many *gelaterie*, or visit the pigeons and cart horses that congregate in the Piazza della Signoria.

Older children might enjoy the climb to the top of the campanile or the dome in the cathedral, if they can tolerate over 400 steps each. Consider a visit to one of the more offbeat museums, such as the 'Specola' Natural History Museum (www. msn.unifi.it), Via Romana 17, in the Oltrarno neighbourhood; the Anthropology Museum, Via del Proconsolo 12; the Museum of Mineralogy, the Botanical Museum and the Museum of Geology and Palaeontology, Via La Pira 4. The Stibbert Museum (www.museostibbert.it) is a little out of town, but the superb armour collections spark the imagination.

Particularly good for children is the Museo dei Ragazzi (Children's Museum; www.museoragazzi.it), a scheme that has created interactive learning spaces for youngsters across Florence with the aim of getting them involved in the art and history of the city. There are multimedia stations across the historic centre, notably at the Palazzo Vecchio (Piazza della Signoria), in the Museo di Storia della Scienza (Museum of the History of Science) and the Museo Stibbert. Highlights include encounters with historical figures such as Galileo and Vasari through lively narrations.

Horse-drawn carriage rides are a popular diversion

Calendar of Events

February/March Shrove Tuesday: a low-key event in Florence, but nearby villages celebrate with fireworks and processions, the most notable of which are in Viareggio.

25 March Annunciation Day: celebrated with a small fair in Piazza della Santissima Annunziata.

March/April Easter Sunday Scoppio del Carro (Explosion of the Cart): an outdoor oxen-drawn cart full of fireworks in Piazza del Duomo is set off by a mechanical dove that travels by wire from the cathedral's high altar at midday mass.

23 May Ascension Day, Festa del Grillo (Festival of the Cricket): fair in Cascine Park popular with children. Crickets in tiny cages sold to be set free.

Mid-May to late June Maggio Musicale (Musical May): prestigious programme of opera, ballet and concerts throughout the city by local and visiting artists (see www.maggiofiorentino.com).

16–17 June San Ranieri Historical Regatta, Pisa. The city's patron saint is celebrated by illuminations, processions and races along the river.

Last Sunday in June Il Gioco del Ponte, Pisa. Twelve teams take part in a tug-of-war on the Ponte di Mezzo across the Arno.

June to September Estate Fiesolana: summer festival of music, ballet and theatre in hilltop town of Fiesole.

24 June Feast of St John the Baptist, patron saint of Florence, celebrated with fireworks. Calcio in Costume: historical rowdy football game in 16th-century costume in Piazza Santa Croce, preceded by an elaborate parade.

Late June/early July Florence Dance Festival: an extravaganza of dancing in venues throughout the city. Takes place over three weeks. For further details of events, tel: (055) 289 276.

2 July and 16 August Palio di Siena: historic pageant and raucous horse race in Siena's beautiful Piazza del Campo.

7 September Festa delle Rificolone (Festival of the Chinese Lanterns): evening procession with torches and paper lanterns on Ponte San Niccolò.

September to December Main opera season, with performances at the Teatro Communale, Corso Italia 16.

EATING OUT

The emphasis in Tuscan cuisine is on straightforward, simply prepared country *cucina povera* (meaning 'poor man's fare'). This comprises few seasonings, no elaborate sauces and the full flavour of primary ingredients from the bounty of Tuscany's fertile land.

The staples of the Tuscan kitchen are olive oil and bread. The olive oil produced in Tuscany is commonly extra virgin and is widely regarded as the finest in the world – dark green in colour, with a rich, peppery flavour. Tuscan olive oil is used in varying degrees on everything from soup to salad.

Your first taste of traditional crusty Tuscan bread will immediately tell you it contains no salt (and is not eaten with butter). This tradition persists from the Middle Ages, when salt was a luxury item. Bread is served with every meal, and is a basic ingredient in many dishes.

Where and When to Eat

The streets of the historic centre are packed with cafés and bars where you can buy a beverage, snack or quick lunch to enjoy while standing at the bar or seated, or to take away. (Sitting at a table will cost more, while sitting out-side can be twice, or even three times, as expensive.) Another option is the *tavola calda* (hot table), a self-service café where you can choose from a selection of pre-prepared dishes (these alternatives can be good for lunch, but those that cater to tourists usually offer mediocre, though often convenient, meals).

Local specialities

Italian cooking is essentially regional. Each of the country's 20 regions has its own unique specialities rarely found outside its bound-aries, and the terminology may vary for similar dishes.

Enjoying a romantic lunch alfresco

Restaurants range from an expensive *ristorante* to a slightly more modestly priced family *trattoria*. Cover *(coperto)* and service *(servizio)* charges are almost always included, but if not, leave 10 or 15 percent for the waiter. Many *trattorie* offer a three-course, fixed-price *menu turistico* (one 'course' may be a vegetable side dish), which is often a good deal, especially at lunchtime for those who don't want full-portioned dishes.

Breakfast *(prima colazione)* is usually included in the price of accommodation, and almost every hotel offers a buffet, with rolls, fresh fruit, yogurt, cereal, homemade pastries, juice and coffee. It is served usually between 7.30 and 10am.

Lunch *(pranzo*, or *colazione)* is served from 12.30 to 2.30pm, though a limited number of places in Florence's centre will serve food throughout the entire afternoon. Cafés will always provide something to fill the gaps.

Dinner *(cena)* begins at around 7.30pm, and is traditionally a fully fledged affair of four courses.

Pizza made with the freshest ingredients

What to Eat

As in the rest of Italy, restaurants offer four courses: *antipasti* (appetisers), *primo* (the first course, which is soup, pasta and, occasionally, risotto), *secondo* (the second course of meat, game or fish, usually grilled or roasted, and served unaccompanied) and *dolci* (dessert). *Contorni* (optional side dishes) are ordered separately and arrive with the entrée.

Antipasti

As well as the usual, such as *antipasto misto* (a table offering a mixed spread of starters, sometimes 'self-service') and *melone con prosciutto* (cantaloupe with thinly sliced, cured ham), to be eaten during the summer when cantaloupe is in season, look out for Tuscan specialities such as *prosciutto con fichi* (prosciutto with fresh figs), *crostini* (toast-rounds topped with chopped chicken livers, anchovies, capers, etc) or *fettunta* (toasted country bread rubbed with garlic and drizzled with olive oil). This is unfussy farmer's fare and it very rarely disappoints.

Primi

There are some excellent pasta possibilities. Typically Tuscan are *pappardelle alla lepre* (broad noodles, usually home-made, with a tomato-based sauce of wild hare), as well as *spaghetti*, *penne* and *strozzipreti* (a 'priest strangler' of pasta, cheese and spinach, usually baked in the oven), dressed in a simple tomato sauce. Some restaurants will serve half portions *(mezza porzione)* of pasta upon request.

First-course non-pasta options are *polenta ai cinghiali* (a kind of cornmeal porridge dressed with a wild boar ragout), *panzanella* (a refreshing summertime salad of bread with tomato, red onion, basil and cucumber), *risotto ai funghi porcini* (slow-cooked rice with porcini mushrooms), and a speciality of *cacciucco* (a rich fish stew in red wine, tomato and peppers) that can pass as an entrée.

Traditional Tuscan soups include *pappa al pomodoro* (tomato soup thickened with bread), *ribollita* (a filling 'twice boiled' bread-based vegetable soup) and *la minestra* (a seasonal vegetable soup sometimes with pasta).

Secondi

Every visitor to Florence ought to try the famous *bistecca alla fiorentina*, a huge, charcoal-grilled T-bone steak, served with lemon or drizzled with olive oil, at least once. Each steak is at least 2cm (1in) thick and weighs 600–800g (21–28oz), charred and crispy outside, rare and tender inside. It's sold by weight, and is not inexpensive. It is common for two people to share one *bistecca*.

Well-presented fare

Another classic Florentine main course is *trippa alla fiorentina*, which is tripe, cut into thin strips, gently fried in olive oil with onion. This can also be found at tripe stalls across the city.

Also on the menu are *fegato alla fiorentina* (sautéed liver with sage or rosemary), *arista* (roast loin of pork with rosemary and garlic), *fritto misto* (fried chicken and lamb with vegetables; this plate often includes calves' brains), *peposo* (beef stewed in a black pepper and tomato-based sauce) and *stracotto* (tender beef stewed with red wine and tomato).

Chicken turns up on the Tuscan dinner table, but Tuscans love game while in season, and they are more inclined to appreciate pigeon *(piccione)* and pheasant *(fagiano)*. You will find this game roasted *(arrosto)*, stewed *(in umido)* or simply grilled *(alla griglia)*. Simple preparation is always key in *cucina toscana*.

A few restaurants specialise in fish and seafood. Fish entrées from Tuscany's port city of Livorno might include *baccalà alla livornese* (a salted cod, tomato and garlic-based stew), but will simply follow the market's offerings.

Contorni

In Italy, vegetables *(verdure)* are ordered and charged for separately. Try *carciofini fritti* (fried baby artichokes), or grilled mushrooms such as porcini *(funghi* or *porcini alla griglia)*. Typ-

Traditional biscuits

ical Tuscan side dishes include *fagioli all'uccelletto* (boiled white beans sautéed with tomato and sage), *fagioli al fiasco* (same ingredients, but stewed) and *fagioli all'olio* (boiled white beans, seasoned with olive oil, salt and pepper, and eaten at room temperature). *Insalata mista* (a mixed side salad) is usually good, but don't expect this to be included with any meal.

Dolci

Generally, desserts do not hold the same importance in Italy as they do in some other cuisines. Fresh fruit *(frutta di stagione)* or a fruit salad *(macedonia)* made of fresh fruit and ice cream *(gelato)* are the most common desserts. *Biscottini di Prato* (also known as *cantuccini*) are hard almond biscuits that you soften by dipping into a glass of *vin santo*, a sweet dessert wine.

The summer heat in Florence can be overwhelming. A bewildering choice of delicious ice creams *(gelati)* can be found in the city's many *gelaterie*.

A selection of luxurious *gelati*

What to Drink

Thirst-quenchers range from good Italian beers *(birra)* to summertime iced tea, peach- or lemon-flavoured *(tè freddo alla pesca* or *al limone)*, a non-alcoholic bitter *(amaro)*, freshly squeezed fruit juices *(spremuta)* and iced espresso *(caffè freddo)*. For children there's orangeade or lemonade *(aranciata* or *limonata)*. There's always the alternative of mineral water *(acqua minerale)*, still or carbonated *(naturale* or *gasata)*. Florence's tap water is heavily chlorinated, but is safe, albeit unpleasant, to drink.

The traditional **wine** of Tuscany is Chianti, probably the best-known of all Italian wines. For many, Italian wine *is*

Frothy cappuccino

Chianti – a basic pressing made from the Sangiovese grape. After a brief period of dormancy, Chianti production has experienced a resurgence of popularity and sales, and is once again considered one of Europe's premier wines.

Quality and price vary, but it's generally all of good – sometimes superb – quality. The official, Consortium-designated Chianti region stretches from Florence to Siena, entitling producers there to bear the seal of the *Gallo Nero* (black rooster). Seals with a gold border indicate a *Chianti Classico Riserva*, meaning that that vintage was aged a year longer before it was bottled.

Consider joining an organised tour of the finest Chianti cellars. The tours take in Tuscany's gorgeous rural scenery, a few attractions on the way, and usually run from July to October (check with tourist information offices, *see page 128*).

Tuscany produces a number of other good, light non-Chianti reds, including *Brolio, Aleatico di Portoferraio* (from the Isle of Elba), *Vino Nobile di Montepulciano* (a stronger full-bodied red) and a fine aged red, *Brunello di Montalcino*.

Among the few Tuscan white wines are the excellent dry *Montecarlo*, *Vernaccia di San Gimignano* and the mellow *Bianco dell'Elba*.

End your meal with a small glass of *vin santo* ('holy wine'), a deep amber-coloured sweet wine. Or choose from a local *grappa* (a distillate of grape must) or *limoncello*, a home-made lemon-infused vodka served ice-cold.

An after-meal **espresso** *(un caffè)* is also available in decaffeinated form *(decaffinato)*. You can order it short, long, *macchiato* ('stained' with a dot of steamed milk) or just *normale*, black. Ordering *cappuccino* after 11am marks you as a tourist, but waiters are accustomed to the request of after-dinner cappuccinos by now (ordering coffee together with your dinner remains taboo). For a greater ratio of water with your coffee, order a *caffè americano*.

Picnics

For a breath of air, make up a picnic lunch and head for the hills of Fiesole, the Boboli Garden or the terrace of San Miniato al Monte in the area of Piazzale Michelangelo. The only central square providing shade is Santo Spirito, near the Pitti Palace. Buy fresh fruit and bread from the market, then find one of the many Florentine delicatessens (*pizzicheria* or *salumeria*) or small grocers (*alimentari*) who stock a wide range of food and drink (including mineral water and soft drinks), and often sell sandwich rolls (*panini*).

Delicious foods to try include *finocchiona*, Tuscany's fennel-studded salami, and the wide range of Italian hams, salamis, *mortadella*, sausages and other cold meats. Cheese is also an important Italian picnic ingredient. Varieties to try include *stracchino*, *pecorino* (a tangy sheep's-milk cheese), *ricotta*, *provola* (smoked or fresh), *gorgonzola*, *parmigiano* and *grana*.

To Help You Order…

A table for one/ two/three please	**Un tavolo per una persona/ per due/per tre**
I would like…	**Vorrei…**
The bill please	**Il conto per favore**
What would you recommend?	**Cosa ci consiglia?**

…and Read the Menu

aglio	garlic	**maiale**	pork
agnello	lamb	**manzo**	beef
aragosta	lobster	**melanzane**	aubergine
basilico	basil	**olio**	oil
birra	beer	**olive**	olives
bistecca	beefsteak	**pane**	bread
burro	butter	**panna**	cream
calamari	squid	**patate**	potatoes
carciofi	artichokes	**peperoni**	peppers
cavallo	horse	**pesce**	fish
cinghiale	wild boar	**piselli**	peas
cipolle	onions	**pollo**	chicken
coniglio	rabbit	**polpo/pólipo**	octopus
cozze	mussels	**pomodori**	tomatoes
fagioli	beans	**prosciutto**	ham
fagiolini	green beans	**riso**	rice
finocchio	fennel	**salsiccie**	sausages
formaggio	cheese	**spinaci**	spinach
frittata	omelette	**tonno**	tuna
frutti di mare	seafood	**uova**	eggs
funghi	mushrooms	**verdure**	vegetables
gamberetti	shrimps	**vino**	wine
gamberi	prawns	**vitello**	veal
gelato	ice cream	**vongole**	clams
insalata	salad	**zucchini**	courgettes
lumache	snails	**zuppa**	soup

HANDY TRAVEL TIPS

An A–Z Summary of Practical Information

A

ACCOMMODATION (*alloggio*; See also CAMPING, YOUTH HOSTELS and the list of Recommended Hotels on page 132)

Florence offers a wide range of accommodation, from luxury hotels set in Renaissance palazzos, through more modest hotels, to former *pensioni*. Rental villas (and apartments within villas) are available just outside of Florence. The following website will help with additional information: www.agriturismo.regione.toscana.it.

Hotels are graded from one to five stars. The Florence Tourist Board (APT; see also TOURIST INFORMATION; www.firenzeturismo. it; email: info@firenzeturismo.it) publishes an annual list of hotels that details prices and facilities. During the high season between March and October, Florence becomes very crowded and accommodation is at a premium. Book as far in advance as possible for this period.

If you find yourself in Florence without a hotel reservation, head for the Informazioni Turistiche Alberghiere (ITA) office in the Santa Maria Novella railway station (tel: 055-282 893; daily 8.45am–8pm); they will find you a room within your price range.

Florence is expensive, on a par with the major European cities. Prices must be clearly displayed in the reception area and in the rooms. Breakfast (often an abundant buffet, but sometimes just rolls and coffee) is almost always included in the room rate.

Do you have any vacancies?	**Avete camere libere?**
I'd like a single/double room	**Vorrei una camera singola/matrimoniale**
...with bath/shower/ private toilet	**...con bagno/doccia/ gabinetto privato**
What's the rate per night/week?	**Qual è il prezzo per una notte/una settimana?**

AIRPORTS (aeroporti)

The largest international airport in the vicinity of Florence is in Pisa. British Airways (www.ba.com) flies direct to Pisa from London Gatwick, and the budget airlines easyJet (www.easyjet.com) and Ryanair (www.ryanair.com) fly direct from Gatwick and London Stansted respectively.

Aeroporto Galileo Galilei (www.pisa-airport.com) is about 81km (51 miles) west of Florence. Facilities include a self-service restaurant, bar/café, post office, bank, ATM, 24-hour currency-exchange machine, tourist information desk and car-hire desks. For flight information, call (050) 849 300 between 8am and 10pm. A regular train service (www.ferroviedellostato.it) links Florence to Pisa Centrale station, which can be reached from the airport by train (infrequent connections), bus or taxi. There is also a coach (www.terra vision.it) that runs directly from Pisa Airport to Florence SMN station. All tickets can be purchased at the airport.

Florence's own small but growing airport – **Aeroporto Amerigo Vespucci** – is at Perètola, 5km (3 miles) northwest of the city: www.aeroporto.firenze.it. It handles domestic as well as daily flights to and from major European cities. The main carrier between the UK and Perètola is Meridiana (www.meridiana.it). For flight information, call (055) 306 1300 from 7.30am to 11.30pm. To report or check on lost baggage, call (055) 306 1302. A regular 30-minute bus service, 'Vola in Bus', connects the airport with the SITA bus station in central Florence every 20 minutes; or take a taxi for approximately €15 to midtown destinations.

Could you please take these bags to the bus/train/ taxi, please?	**Mi porti queste valige fino all'autobus/ al treno/al taxi, per favore?**
What time does the train for Florence leave?	**A che ora parte il treno per Firenze?**

Another option is to fly to Bologna's **G. Marconi Airport** (www.bologna-airport.it), 66km (41 miles) north of Florence. This route is served by British Airways, and these flights are often cheaper than on the Pisa route. Ryanair also flies to Bologna daily from the UK.

In Bologna a shuttle bus operates between the airport (just outside the main terminal building) and Bologna Centrale railway station. Trains run about twice hourly and the journey to Florence takes just over an hour.

B

BICYCLE HIRE (noleggio biciclette)

In an effort to reduce congestion and pollution, more and more of the flat *centro storico* is being closed to vehicles. The city council has provided bicycles at parking areas throughout the city and charges a nominal fee to use them for as much time as you like.

For better-quality bicycles you can try Florence By Bike, Via San Zanobi 120/122r, tel/fax: (055) 488 992, www.florencebybike.it, where you can also hire motor scooters. The company's multilingual staff organise full tours in and out of the city.

BUDGETING FOR YOUR TRIP

Hotels (double room with bath, including tax and service, high-season rates): 5-star from €450, 4-star €250–450, 3-star €150–250, 2-star €120–150, 1-star under €120.

Meals and drinks: Continental breakfast €8; lunch/dinner in fairly good establishment €20–40; coffee served at a table €2–3.50, served at the bar €1. Also at the bar: bottle of beer €1.50–2; soft drinks €1.50–3; aperitif €3 and up.

Museums: admission fees range from approximately €2 for the small church museums to between €6.50 and €10 for some of the major collections.

Entertainment: cinema €8, concert €15–25, opera €15–50.

C

CAMPING (campeggio)

There is only one campsite convenient to the centre of Florence, with 240 pitches set on a pleasant hillside above the river east of Piazzale Michelangelo (30 minutes' walk from the Uffizi). Contact Campeggio Italiani e Stranieri (Camping Michelangelo), Viale Michelangelo 80, 50125 Florence, tel: (055) 681 1977, fax: (055) 689 348, www.camping.it. Reservations required.

There are several other campsites around the fringes of the city, and one in Fiesole: Campeggio Panoramico (Camping Panorama), Via Peramonda l, Fiesole, tel: (055) 599 069. For details, contact the tourist office. Area Flog Pogetto, a service area for campers, with water and electric points, is located on Via M. Mercati 24/b, tel: (055) 481 285. There is also a free emergency campsite with very limited facilities for stranded backpackers: the Area di Sosta, on the edge of town. It is open in summer only, and the location sometimes changes from year to year. Ask at the tourist information office for the address of the current site.

May we camp here?	**Possiamo campeggiare qui?**
Is there a campsite near here?	**C'è un campeggio qui vicino?**
We have a tent/caravan (trailer).	**Abbiamo una tenda/una roulotte.**

CAR HIRE (autonoleggio; See also DRIVING)

Driving in Florence is not a good idea: cars are prevented from going into much of the city centre, and the bewildering array of dead-ends and one-way streets make it difficult to navigate. Add to that the problem of parking (usually only for residents) and the fact that it is a small place and hence easy to get everywhere on foot, and there is really little point in going through all the hassle.

If you do need to hire a care, however, prices start from around €40 a day. Reliable firms include: **Auto Europa**, Via il Prato 47r, tel: (050) 506 883; **Avis**, Borgo Ognissanti 128r, tel: (055) 213 629; **Hertz**, Via Maso Finiguerra 33r, tel: (055) 282 260; and **Maxirent**, Borgo Ognissanti 133r; tel: (055) 265 4207.

I'd like to rent a car.	**Vorrei noleggiare una macchina.**
...for one day/a week	**...per un giorno/una settimana**
I want full insurance.	**Voglio l'assicurazione completa.**

CLIMATE

Summer is often oppressively hot and sticky (the hills surrounding Florence capture the heat and humidity), while midwinter can be unpleasantly cold. The wettest months are from October to April. The best times to visit are in spring and autumn, when temperatures are less extreme, but May and September have become extremely popular (and crowded) months to visit.

		J	F	M	A	M	J	J	A	S	O	N	D
°C	max	9	12	16	20	24	29	32	31	28	21	14	10
	min	2	2	5	5	12	15	17	17	15	11	6	3
°F	max	48	53	59	68	75	84	89	88	82	70	57	50
	min	35	36	40	46	53	59	62	61	59	52	43	37

CLOTHING

Light clothes are best for coping with the summer heat, but you'll want a sweater or jacket on the cool evenings in spring and autumn. In winter you will need warm clothes, a waterproof jacket and an umbrella. Comfortable walking shoes for those cobbled streets are highly recommended. Remember that Florence's churches are places of worship as well as works of art and architecture, so dress respectably if you intend to visit them – shorts, miniskirts and bare shoulders are frowned upon, and sometimes forbidden.

CRIME AND SAFETY

Florence is a fairly safe city, but you should take the usual precautions against theft – don't carry large amounts of cash, and leave your valuables in the hotel safe (not in your room, unless there is a room safe). Never leave your bags or valuables in view in a parked car; and never leave your bags in a car boot overnight, even if out of sight. The only real danger is from possible pickpockets, especially in crowded areas, busy markets and on public buses. If you have a shoulder bag, wear it across your body – it's harder to snatch.

Any theft or loss must be reported immediately to the police; make sure you obtain a copy of the report in order to comply with your travel insurance. If your passport is lost or stolen, inform your consulate immediately.

I want to report a theft.	**Voglio denunciare un furto.**
My wallet/passport/ticket has been stolen.	**Mi hanno rubato il portafoglio/ il passaporto/il biglietto.**
I've lost my passport/ wallet/bag/purse.	**Ho perso il passaporto/ il portafoglio/la borsa/ la borsetta.**

CUSTOMS AND ENTRY REQUIREMENTS

For citizens of EU countries, a valid passport or identity card is needed to enter Italy for stays of up to 90 days. Citizens of Australia, New Zealand and the US also require only a valid passport.

Visas (permesso di soggiorno). For stays of more than 90 days a special visa or residence permit is required. Visa regulations change from time to time; for full information on passport and visa regulations check with the Italian Embassy in your country.

Free exchange of non-duty-free goods for personal use is allowed between EU countries. For residents of non-EU countries, restrictions when returning home are as follows:

	Cigarettes		Cigars		Tobacco	Alcohol		Wine		Beer
Canada	200	and	50	and	200g	1.14l	or	1.5l	or	8.5l
New Zealand	200	or	50	or	250g	1l	and	4.5l	or	4.5l
South Africa	400	and	50	and	250g	1l	and	2l		
US	200	or	100	or	2kg	1l	and	1l	or	1l

Currency restrictions. Tourists may bring an unlimited amount of Italian or foreign currency into the country. On departure you must declare any currency beyond the equivalent of €10,300, so it's wise to declare sums exceeding this amount when you arrive.

I've nothing to declare.	**Non ho niente da dichiarare.**
It's for my personal use.	**È per mio uso personale.**

D

DRIVING

Motorists planning to take their vehicle into Italy need a full driving licence, an International Motor Insurance Certificate and a Vehicle Registration Document. A green insurance card is not a legal requirement, but it is strongly recommended. Foreign visitors must display an official nationality sticker, and, if coming from the UK or Ireland, headlights must be adjusted for driving on the right. The use of seatbelts is obligatory; fines for noncompliance are stiff. A red warning triangle must be carried in case of breakdown. Motorcycle riders must wear helmets. Documents must be carried at all times.

Driving conditions. Drive on the right, pass on the left. Give way to traffic coming from the right. Speed limits: 50kmh (30mph) in town, 90kmh (55mph) on motorways and 130kmh (80mph) on highways.

Traffic police *(polizia stradale)*. Italian traffic police are authorised to impose on-the-spot fines for speeding and other traffic offences, such as driving while intoxicated or stopping in a no-stopping zone. All cities, and many towns and villages, have signs posted at the outskirts indicating the telephone number of the local traffic police headquarters or Carabinieri (see POLICE). Police have recently become stricter about speeding.

Should you be involved in a road accident, dial **112** for the *carabinieri*. If your car is stolen or broken into, contact the Urban Police Headquarters *(Questura)* in Florence at Via Zara 2, and get a copy of their report for your insurance claim.

In the event of a breakdown, find a telephone and dial **116**. This will put you in touch with the ACI (Automobile Club d'Italia), the national automobile organisation. About every 2km (1½ miles or so) on the *autostrada* there's an emergency call box marked 'SOS'.

Driving in Florence. Taking a car to Florence is not worth the hassle. The centre of Florence (within the circle of avenues or *viali* that surround it on both sides of the River Arno) is a restricted ZTL area (*zona traffico limitato* – limited traffic zone). Between 7.30am and 6.30pm Monday–Saturday, only residents with special permits on their windscreens are allowed into this zone.

Traffic police are usually stationed at the major entry roads to stop anyone without a permit. Tourists may enter to offload baggage and passengers at their hotel (carry confirmation from your hotel to facilitate entry); you must then go and park outside the ZTL. If you can speak Italian, ask a policeman for directions, as the one-way system is rather complex.

Parking (*parcheggio*). Even if you make it into the city centre after 6.30pm, or on a Sunday, it is virtually impossible to park on the street, but you can pay to park in one of the 70-plus official car parks. Parking in the street is generally reserved for residents 8am–8pm.

Apart from the city-centre parking places, there are others at Porta Romana (left bank), the Cascine (Piazza Vittorio Veneto) and Fortezza da Basso (Viale Filippo Strozzi). A smaller – but convenient – car park is located in Piazza Libertà.

There is a very new system for parking on some streets indicated by blue painted markers. Between 8am and 8pm you can pre-pay an estimated time using an often semi-hidden meter marked with a white 'P' on a blue background; place the issued ticket inside your windscreen.

If you park your car on the street overnight in the centre of Florence, be extremely careful to heed the restrictions posted on parking signs. Fines are very heavy, and the city is well equipped to remove illegally parked cars and tow them to the car pound (Via Olmatelo in the area called Novoli). If this should happen, call (or ask your hotel to call) the municipal police, tel: (055) 308 249, to

Curva pericolosa	Dangerous bend/curve
Deviazione	Detour
Divieto di sorpasso	No passing
Divieto di sosta	No stopping
Lavori in corso	Roadworks/Men working
Pericolo	Danger
Rallentare	Slow down
Senso vietato/unico	No entry/One-way street
Vietato l'ingresso	No entry
Zona pedonale	Pedestrian zone
ZTL	Limited traffic zone

locate your car. You'll need to go there in person with documents and pay a stiff fine to get it back. It is every visitor's nightmare.

E

ELECTRICITY

220V/50Hz AC is standard in Italy. An adaptor *(una presa complementare)* for Continental-style sockets will be needed; American 110V appliances also require a transformer.

EMBASSIES AND CONSULATES

In Florence:
South Africa (consulate): Piazza Salterelli 1, tel: (055) 281 863.
UK (consulate): Lungarno Corsini 2, tel: (055) 284 133.
US (consulate): Lungarno A. Vespucci 38, tel: (055) 266 95.1

In Rome:
Australia (HC): Via Antonio Bosio 5, tel: (06) 852 721, www.italy.embassy.gov.au.
Canada (HC): Via Zara 30, tel: (06) 445 981, www.canada.it.
New Zealand (embassy): Via Zara 28, tel: (06) 441 7171, www.nzembassy.com.
Republic of Ireland (embassy): Piazza di Campitelli 3, tel: (06) 697 9121, www.ambasciata-irlanda.it.
UK (embassy): Via XX Settembre 80a, tel: (06) 4220 0001, www.britain.it.

EMERGENCIES

If you don't speak Italian, find a local resident to help you or talk to the English-speaking operator on the telephone assisted service, tel: **170**.

Police   **112**
General emergency   **113**

Fire   **115**
Paramedics   **118**

Please, can you place an emergency call to the...?	**Per favore, può fare una telefonata d'emergenza...?**
police	**alla polizia**
fire brigade	**ai pompieri**
hospital	**all'ospedale**

G

GAY AND LESBIAN TRAVELLERS

Florence historically has been tolerant of gays. There are several gay bars, including Tabasco (Piazza Santa Cecilia 3) and the Piccolo Caffè (Borgo Santa Croce 23r). You may also want to contact ARCI-gay, the national gay rights organisation; tel: (055) 012 3121, www.arcigayfirenze.it.

GETTING THERE

By air. The best deal on scheduled flights is the advanced-purchase fare of a weekday departure, which must be booked at least seven or 14 days in advance, and must include a Saturday night.

From the UK and US, there are scheduled flights from the major cities to the international gateway airports of Rome and Milan, where you can catch a connecting flight to Pisa (80km/50 miles from Florence) or to Florence itself. Non-stop flights from the UK connect London with Pisa and occasionally also with Florence. Ryanair, www.ryanair.com, offers economical, direct flights from London Stansted to Pisa and Bologna 100km (60 miles) from Florence. Easy-Jet, www.easyjet.com, also flies to Pisa.

It is sometimes possible to get a seat on a charter flight on a flight-only basis, and this will generally be cheaper than a high-season ticket on a scheduled flight. However, charters are less flexible, with perhaps only two flights weekly, and there are restrictions attached which should be checked out at the start. Cancellation insurance is recommended.

By road. A coach service runs from London Victoria to Florence. For drivers taking their own vehicles, the fastest route from the UK is via Paris and the A6 Autoroute du Soleil to near Mâcon, then east on the A40 and through the Mont Blanc Tunnel to Turin, Genoa and finally Florence.

By rail. The train journey from London to Florence via Paris takes around 15 hours: 2 hours and 15 minutes from London St Pancras to Paris Gare du Nord on Eurostar, and another 12-hour journey from Paris Bercy to Florence Santa Maria Novella. The Artesia service (www.artesia.eu) leaves Bercy at around 7pm and arrives at Santa Maria Novella at around 7am the next day. It is a pleasant journey, but it is more expensive than flying.

If you are touring Europe by rail, the following passes can be used in Italy: Inter-Rail, Rail Europ Senior, Eurailpass, Eurail Youthpass and other Eurail passes; see www.raileurope.co.uk for booking and details on these passes.

Italian State Railways, www.ferroviedellostato.it, offer fare reductions in certain cases. These are subject to variation, but there are almost always discounts for children and groups available. Ask at any railway station or go to the website for current information. These tickets can be purchased at home or in Italy.

GUIDES AND TOURS *(guide, gite)*

Independent English-speaking guides can be hired through the Tuscan Tourist Guides Society:

AGT Ass., Via Palazzuolo 58/r, tel/fax: (055) 264 5217, www. florencetouristguides.com.

A number of organised two- and three-hour walking tours of the historic centre are less expensive and are an enjoyable and educational way to orientate yourself. Hotels and tourist offices will have details.

Some travel agencies and bus companies offer organised bus tours of the countryside around Florence, including excursions to San Gimignano/Siena or Pisa. Details can be obtained through your hotel, the tourist information office and local travel agencies.

We'd like an English-speaking guide.	**Desideriamo una guida che parla inglese.**
I need an English interpreter.	**Ho bisogno di un interprete d'inglese.**

H

HEALTH AND MEDICAL CARE (see also EMERGENCIES)

EU citizens are entitled to free emergency hospital treatment if they have a European Health Insurance Card (obtainable from a post office before leaving home). You may have to pay part of the price of treatment or medicine; if so, remember to keep receipts so that you can claim a refund when you return home. It is advisable to obtain travel insurance before you leave home to be sure you are covered.

The special social clinic (ASL) for foreigners is *Assistenza Medica A Stranieri In Italia*, Borgognissanti 20, tel: (055) 228 5501 (Mon–Sat

I need a doctor/dentist.	**Ho bisogno di un medico/dentista.**
It hurts here.	**Ho un dolore qui.**
a stomach ache	**un mal di stomaco**
a fever	**la febbre**
sunburn/sunstroke	**una scottatura di sole/ un colpo di sole**

8am–noon and Wed also from 2.30–4.30pm). The American Consulate recommends the English-speaking walk-in clinic of Giorgio Scappini, Via Bonifaciolupi 32, tel: (055) 483 363 or (0330) 774 731.

If you should need the services of an interpreter in a medical situation, contact the Associazione Volontari Ospedalieri, a group of volunteer interpreters who are always on call, and offer their telephone services free; tel: (055) 234 4567.

Most pharmacies *(farmacie)* follow retail hours; the one in the Santa Maria Novella railway station stays open all night. At weekends or on public holidays, the addresses of pharmacists on duty are published in the newspaper *La Nazione* and are posted on every *farmacia* door. In Italy, pharmacists are able to diagnose and prescribe mild medication for which, elsewhere, you would normally need a prescription. If it is not a true emergency, make a visit to a pharmacist instead of the hospital.

Tap water is safe to drink *(potabile)*. There are numerous old drinking fountains in Florence's parks and piazzas.

L

LANGUAGE

English is widely spoken in Florence (especially by the young), and you can get by without a word of Italian, but it is polite to learn at least a few basic phrases.

Local people will welcome and encourage any attempt you make to use their language. When you enter a shop, restaurant or office, the greeting is always *buon giorno* (good morning) or *buona sera* (good afternoon/evening – used from around 1pm onwards). When enquiring, start with *per favore* (please), and for any service rendered say *grazie* (thanks), to which the reply is *prego* (don't mention it, you're welcome). Accompany a handshake with *piacere* (it's a pleasure). A more familiar greeting, used among friends, is *ciao*, which means both 'Hi' and 'See you later'.

M

MAPS

Tourist offices *(see page 128)* can supply free maps of the city centre and also have a useful leaflet, *'Un giorno, a Firenze'* ('A day in Florence') that describes a walking tour around the main sights. The best commercially available map of the city is by the Touring Club Italiano and is available in good bookshops such as Feltrinelli at Via de' Cerretani 30r.

I'd like a street plan of…	**Vorrei una pianta della città…**
I'd like a road map of this region.	**Vorrei una carta stradale di questa regione.**

MEDIA

Newspapers and magazines *(giornali; riviste)*. The Florence-based national newspaper *La Nazione* provides national and international news, features and useful restaurant reviews and entertainment listings. *La Repubblica* also has a Florence edition. You can find newspapers in English at city-centre newsstands. *The International Herald Tribune* is available on the day of publication. A free booklet called *Concierge Information* is available from most hotels and contains a lot of handy information, including museum hours, special museum exhibitions, train and bus timetables, and useful addresses.

Radio and TV *(radio, televisione)*. Italy's state-sponsored TV network, RAI *(Radiotelevisione Italiana)*, broadcasts three TV channels, which compete with six independent channels. All programmes are in Italian, including British and American feature films and imports, which are dubbed. CNN and BBC World are available in most hotels. The airwaves are crammed with Italian-language radio stations, most of them broadcasting popular music.

MONEY

Currency. The official currency used in Italy is the euro (€). Notes are in denominations of 5, 10, 20, 50, 100 and 500 euros; coins in 1 and 2 euros and 1, 2, 5, 10, 20 and 50 cents.

Banks and currency exchange offices. Banking hours are generally Monday–Friday 8.30am–1pm and 2.30–4pm. The exchange offices on Via dei Calzaiuoli, between the Duomo and Piazza della Signoria, are open all day and at weekends. Commission charges can be high, around €2–3 per transaction or according to the amount exchanged; it is almost always posted, often in small print. Taking cash advances from an ATM *(bancomat)* or changing money in a bank usually offers the best exchange rate. Check with your bank at home to make sure that your account is authorised for international withdrawals. Look for correlating symbols on the cash machine and the back of your card. American Express has a full-service office for its clients on Via Dante Aligheri 22/r, near the Duomo.

Travellers' cheques and credit cards. In the main tourist areas, almost everyone accepts travellers' cheques, although you're likely to get a better exchange rate at a bank. You'll usually need your passport to cash a travellers' cheque. Keep your remaining cheques in the hotel safe, if possible. At the very least, be sure to keep your receipt and a list of the serial numbers of the cheques

I want to change some pounds/dollars/ travellers' cheques.	**Desidero cambiare delle sterline/dei dollari/ 'travellers' cheques'**
Can I pay with this credit card?	**Posso pagare con la carta di credito?**
Where is the bank/ATM?	**Dov'è il banco/bancomat?**

in a separate place to facilitate a refund in case of loss or theft. All major credit cards are usually accepted by hotels, restaurants, car-hire firms and other businesses; look for the symbols on the door to be sure. Visa and MasterCard are more widely accepted than American Express.

O

OPENING HOURS

Banks. These are usually open Monday–Friday 8am–1.30pm and 2.30–4pm. Exchange offices at airports and major railway stations are open until late in the evening and on Saturday and Sunday.

Churches generally close for sightseeing at lunchtime, approximately noon–3pm or even later. They discourage tourist visits during Sunday morning services.

Museums and art galleries. Museums and art galleries usually change their hours from one season to the next. They are generally open from 9 or 9.30am–4pm, and in some cases 5–8pm Tuesday–Saturday and until 1pm on Sunday. Closing day is usually Monday. If Monday is a holiday, some museums and galleries close the following day. Check times locally before you set out. Useful websites to consult are www.firenzemusei.it and www.polo museale.firenze.it.

Shops. Although many of the large shops and supermarkets now remain open all day *(no-stop* or *orario continuato)*, the majority still adhere to the decades-old Florentine tradition of closing for a long lunch and on Monday mornings (Wednesday afternoons for food shops). Generally, shop opening hours are: Monday 3.30–7.30pm and Tuesday–Saturday 8.30 or 9.00am–1pm and 3.30 or 4–7 or 8pm. Food shops tend to open earlier than this and close earlier, while clothes shops may do the opposite, often not opening until 10am. Some of the central Florentine shops remain open for some part of Sunday, but many still close on that day. There are a limited number of shops open during the month of August, and if you see a sign that says *chiuso per ferie* with dates, it indicates they are closed for a holiday and usually indicates the date when they will reopen. Good shopping times in Italy are the two legal sales periods *(saldi)*: from the second week of January to the second week of February, and mid-August to mid-September.

P

POLICE *(polizia)*

Florence's city police, the Vigili Urbani, handle traffic and parking and perform other routine tasks. While the officers rarely speak English, they are courteous and helpful towards tourists. The *carabinieri*, a paramilitary force, wear light-brown or blue uniforms with peaked caps, and deal with more serious crimes and demonstrations. Outside town, the Polizia Stradale patrol the highways, issue speeding tickets and assist with breakdowns (see also DRIVING).

Vigili Urbani Headquarters *(Questura)* and Stolen Vehicles Department, Via Zara 2, tel: (055) 49771.

Carabinieri Regional Headquarters (the only station where you're likely to find someone who speaks English): Borgo Ognissanti 48, tel: (055) 24811.

Polizia Stradale (Traffic Police), tel: (055) 577 777.

Polizia Assistenza Turistica (Tourist Police), Via Pietrapiana 50r, tel: (055) 203 911.

Where's the nearest police station?	Dov'è il più vicino punto di polizia?

POST OFFICES

The central post office in Florence is on Via Pellicceria, just south-west of Piazza della Repubblica. You can enter by a back door on Piazza Davanzati. It handles mail, telegrams, telex, fax services (to some but not all countries) and has a tourist information kiosk. Its opening hours are Monday–Friday 8.15am–7pm, Saturday 8.15am–1.30pm.

Most other post offices open from 8.15 or 8.30am–1.30 or 2pm Monday–Friday, until noon on Saturday and on the last day of the month.

Post boxes are red – those marked *per la città* are for destinations within Florence, *per tutte le altre destinazioni* for all other destinations. The blue box is for express international post.

General delivery *(fermo posta)*. If you're going to be in Florence without a secure address, you can receive 'snail' mail at poste restante *(fermo posta)* at the Via Pellicceria post office *(see above)*. Don't forget your passport for identification when you go to pick up mail. Have mail addressed as follows: (Your Name), Fermo Posta, Palazzo delle Poste, 50100 Florence, Italy.

Where's the nearest post office?	**Dov'è l'ufficio postale più vicino?**
Have you received any mail for…?	**C'è posta per…?**
I'd like a stamp for this letter/postcard.	**Desidero un francobollo per questa lettera/cartolina.**

PUBLIC HOLIDAYS *(feste)*

Banks, offices, government institutions, most shops and many museums are closed on national holidays, as well as on the Florentines' local holiday on 24 June, commemorating the town's patron saint,

San Giovanni Battista (St John the Baptist). During the long week-end of 15 August, almost everything in Florence (and Italy) closes, except hotels, a few shops, pharmacies, cafés, restaurants and some of the major tourist attractions. Most make a week (or longer) of it.

1 January	*Capodanno/* *Primo dell'Anno*	New Year's Day
6 January	*Epifania*	Epiphany
25 April	*Festa della Liberazione*	Liberation Day
1 May	*Festa del Lavoro*	Labour Day
24 June	*San Giovanni*	Patron Saint of Florence
15 August	*Ferragosto*	Feast of the Assumption
1 November	*Ognissanti*	All Saints' Day
8 December	*Concezione Immacolata*	Immaculate Conception
25 December	*Natale*	Christmas Day
26 December	*Santo Stefano*	St Stephen's Day

Movable dates:
Pasqua	Easter
Pasquetta/Lunedì di Pasqua	Easter Monday

R

RELIGION *(religione)*

Italy is an overwhelmingly Roman Catholic country, with Catholicism accounting for 83 percent of the population. Mass is celebrated in English in the Duomo every Saturday at 5pm, and in the Church of San Giovanni di Dio, Borgognissanti 16–20, on Sundays and holidays at 10am.

Many other denominations are represented in Florence; for details, contact the tourist information office *(see page 128)*.

In churches, shorts, miniskirts or bare shoulders are not considered respectable.

T

TELEPHONES

The country code for Italy is **39**, and the area code for the city of Florence is **055**. Note that you must dial the 055 prefix even when making local calls within the city of Florence.

You can make local and international calls from the orange public telephones located all over the city, which accept coins. Many also accept phone cards *(scheda telefonica)*, which can be bought from bars, tobacco stands *(tabacchi)* and newsstands, and are available for €5 and €25. There is a convenient Telecom phone centre located at Via Cavour 21/r (7am–11pm), where you can purchase phone cards and find telephone books and usually a free and functioning phone.

To make an international call, dial 00, followed by the country code (**44** for UK, **1** for US), then the area code and number.

If you would like to use a charge card or make a reverse-charge (collect) call, the following are a list of access numbers for your country's toll-free centres. (Note: You must always insert a coin or a card to access a line, even when making a toll-free call.)

To place reverse-charge (collect) calls or operator-assisted calls use the following numbers: **1795** (International); **170** (English-speaking operators). For directory assistance: **1254** (International); **176** (English-speaking operators).

Mobile phones. You will probably find that your mobile phone will work in Italy, although calls will be more expensive than at home. If your phone is 'unlocked' it is easy to buy a local pay-as-you-go SIM card. Reliable firms include Vodaphone Italia and Telecom Italia Mobile (TIM).

| Give me coins/a telephone card, please. | **Per favore, mi dia monette/ una scheda telefonica.** |

TIME DIFFERENCES

Italian time coincides with most of Western Europe – Greenwich Mean Time plus one hour. In summer, an hour is added for Daylight Saving Time.

New York	London	**Florence**	Jo'burg	Sydney
6am	11am	**noon**	1pm	8pm

TIPPING *(la mancia)*

Though a service charge is commonly added to most restaurant bills (look for *servizio incluso*), it is customary to leave a small additional tip. If service charge is not included, 10–15 percent is the norm.

It is also customary to tip bellboys, doormen and lavatory attendants for their service. Taxi drivers do not expect a full 10 percent, and normal practice by Italians is simply to round up the fare.

Thank you, this is for you.	**Grazie, questo è per Lei.**
Keep the change.	**Tenga il resto.**

TOILETS *(gabinetti)*

You will find public toilets in airports, railway and bus stations, museums and art galleries; they are often designated by the sign 'WC'. The men's may be indicated by 'U' *(uomini)*, or 'signori', the ladies' by 'D' *(donne)*, or 'signore'.

Where are the toilets?	**Dove sono i gabinetti?**

TOURIST INFORMATION

The Italian State Tourist Office, or ENIT (www.enit.it), maintains offices in many countries, including:

Canada: 175 Bloor Street, East Suite 907, Toronto, Ontario, M4W 3R8, tel: (416) 925 4882, www.italiantourism.com.

UK: 1 Princes Street, London W1R 2AY, tel: (020) 7408 1254, www.italiantouristboard.co.uk.

US: 500 N. Michigan Avenue, Chicago, IL 60611, tel: (312) 644 0996; 630 Fifth Avenue, New York, NY 10111, tel: (212) 245 5618, www.italiantourism.com.

In Italy, the provincial tourist information offices are the APT (Azienda di Promozione Turistica), www.firenzeturismo.it, email: info@firenzeturismo.it. They have helpful English-speaking staff, and can provide free maps and general advice and information, as well as provide advice on and booking for accommodation. The APT offices in Florence and nearby are listed below:

Florence: Via A. Manzoni 16, tel: (055) 523 320, fax: (055) 234 6286 (Monday–Friday 9am–1pm).

The following are more central:

Via Cavour 1/r, tel: (055) 290 832 (Monday–Saturday 8.30am–6.30pm, Sunday 8.30am–1.30pm).

Borgo S. Croce 29/r, tel: (055) 234 0444 (Monday–Saturday 9am–7pm, until 5pm during winter, Sunday 9am–2pm).

Piazza Stazione 4, tel: (055) 212 245 (Monday–Saturday 8.30am–7pm, Sunday 8.30am–2pm).

For details on museums in Florence and opening times, see www.polomuseale.firenze.it.

Fiesole: Via Portigiani 3, tel: (055) 598 720 (Monday–Saturday 10am–6pm).

Pisa: Piazza del Duomo, tel: (050) 560 464 (Monday–Saturday 9am–6pm, Sun 10.30am–4.30pm).

Siena: Piazza del Campo 56, tel: (0577) 280 551 (daily 9am–7pm).

TRANSPORT

Buses. The orange ATAF buses, www.ataf.net, provide a cheap and efficient way of getting around the city and its suburbs (although in the pedestrian-only centre, almost everything is within walking distance). Before you board, buy your ticket from shops and newsstands displaying an orange *Bigletti Abbonamenti Ataf Qui* ('bus passes here'); stamp it in the yellow box on the bus (ATAF officials periodically conduct spot checks to make sure tickets have been stamped; they impose stiff fines on ticket-holders who have not stamped their tickets, no excuses accepted). Tickets are valid for 1, 2 or 24 hours, and you can make as many journeys as you like, as long as they begin within the period of validity (you only punch the ticket once, on the first bus you use). Tourists can also buy 3-, 5- and 7-day passes. For details of timetables and routes, ask at the ATAF information office outside the railway station or at Piazza del Duomo 57/r.

A number of other bus companies provide inter-city services to destinations further afield, including Siena, Perugia, Rome and Milan. The main companies include SITA, tel: (055) 47821 or (800) 373 760, www.sitabus.it, whose station and information office is on Viale dei Cadorna 105, and Lazzi, tel: (055) 215 155, www.lazzi.it, in Piazza Stazione; they are on opposites sides of the main railway station.

Taxis. Taxis can be picked up at ranks in the main city squares, or called by telephone (tel: 055-4798 or 055-4242) but not hailed. Fares are recorded on the meter, and there are extra charges for luggage, radio calls, Sunday and late-night trips. It is normal practice to round up the fare.

Trains. The Italian State Railway, FS (Ferrovie dello Stato, www.ferroviedellostato.it), has an excellent rail network. Florence's Santa Maria Novella station is well designed and efficient, with regular services to Rome, Milan, Venice (to name but a few) and other European cities. In addition to the information office, there are a number of computerised information points, where you can get train times and fares from a touch-screen terminal. Large postings of *arrivi* (arrivals) and *partenze* (departures) are especially helpful. Prices are reasonable, particularly those for second-class travel. To pay with a credit card, look for the credit-card sticker in the window to make sure you're standing in the right queue. Some ticket machines take credit cards as well as cash. Be aware of the infamous Italian *sciopero* or train strikes (less frequent these days than in the past) that can last from a few hours to a few days. Try to check with your hotel before going to the station, as strikes are always announced and publicised in the paper and on the news the day before, if not sooner.

When's the next bus/train to…?	**Quando parte il prossimo autobus/treno per…?**
single (one-way)	**andata**
return (round-trip)	**andata e ritorno**
first/second class	**prima/seconda classe**
What's the fare to…?	**Qual'è la tariffa per…?**
I'd like to make a seat reservation.	**Vorrei prenotare un posto.**

TRAVELLERS WITH DISABILITIES

Florence is not an easy city for disabled travellers. Many of the more popular attractions are equipped with ramps for wheelchair access, but public transport is a problem, as are hotels, restaurants and most minor attractions. Contact a tourist information office for details about accessible hotels, galleries and museums, and for addresses of Italian associations for the disabled.

WEBSITES AND INTERNET ACCESS

Websites are given throughout the book; of the general sites the most useful are:

www.enit.it – Italian Tourist Board
www.firenzeturismo.it – Florence Tourism
www.firenzemusei.it and **www.polomuseale.firenze.it** – collective sites for the major museums
www.ataf.net – local transport

There are many internet cafés located all over Florence. Internet Train (www.internettrain.it) has several locations in Florence, generally open daily between 10am and 11pm. It also offers scanning, printing and fax services. The most central branch is on Via dell'Oriuolo.

Most hotels offer email access, too. Check with them before you arrive.

Y

YOUTH HOSTELS *(ostelli della gioventù)*

The Italian Youth Hostel Association (Associazione Italiana Alberghi per la Gioventù; www.ostellionline.org) has one hostel in a converted villa on the outskirts of Florence, a 30-minute bus trip from the centre in Fiesole: Ostello Europa Villa Camerata, Viale A. Righi 4, tel: (055) 601 451, fax: (055) 610 300. In the Tuscan countryside 30km (19 miles) from Florence is the Ostello del Chianti, Via Roma 137, Tavernelle Val di Pesa, tel: (055) 805 0265. Contact your national youth hostel association before departure to obtain an international membership card.

There are several other hostels in Florence, some more centrally located than the Hostelling International one. Ostello Santa Monaca (Via Santa Monaca 6, tel: 055-268 338, www.ostello.it) is in Oltrarno between Santo Spirito and Piazza del Carmine. The new Plus Florence Hostel (Via Santa Caterina d'Alessandra 15, tel: 055-462 8934, www.plusvillages.com), complete with swimming pool, bar, terrace and flat-screen TVs, is located northeast of the station.

Recommended Hotels

During the high season from April to November (the clement months of May/June and September are most popular), accommodation in Florence is at a premium, and you should try to book a room as far in advance as possible. In fact, reservations are always strongly recommended, especially for the smaller, lower-priced hotels (with lots of conventions and trade fairs, Florence can fill up even when not expected in off months). However, if you do arrive in Florence without a reservation, the ITA office at Santa Maria Novella railway station will find a room for you *(see page 106)*.

As a basic guide, the symbols below indicate published rack rates per night for a standard double room with bath, including all taxes, service and breakfast. Some hotels discount during the low season, so it is always worth trying to bargain.

€€€€   over 300 euros
€€€   170–300 euros
€€   120–170 euros
€   under 120 euros

CENTRO STORICO (CENTRE)

Beacci Tornabuoni €€€ *Via dei Tornabuoni 3, 50123 Florence, tel: (055) 212 645, fax: (055) 283 594, www.hoteltornabuoni.it.* Classic Florentine *pensione*-like hotel on high floor of a 14th-century palazzo on the city's premier designer-lined shopping street. Old-fashioned elegance with a homely atmosphere and new owners. 29 rooms.

Bernini Palace €€€€ *Piazza San Firenze 29, 50122 Florence, tel: (055) 288 621, fax: (055) 268 272, www.baglionihotels.com.* Atmospheric hotel in a centuries-old palazzo at the back of the Palazzo Vecchio, popular with businessmen for its excellent location and fine service. 75 rooms.

Brunelleschi €€€€ *Piazza Santa Elizabetta 3, 50122 Florence, tel: (055) 27370, fax: (055) 219 653, www.hotelbrunelleschi.it.* Built on Roman foundations, this hotel has its own small medieval museum, and incorporates the adjoining Torre della Pagliazza into the premises – all on its own tiny little piazza in the shadow of the Duomo. 96 rooms.

Helvetia & Bristol €€€€ *Via dei Pescioni 2l, 50123 Florence, tel: (055) 26651, fax: (055) 288 353, www.royaldemeure.com.* A small but grand hotel, with antiques and paintings scattered around the rooms and hallways. The sumptuous rooms have wonderful views and the marble-clad bathrooms are a treat. As well as a pretty winter garden, the hotel has a good restaurant.

Hermitage €€€ *Vicolino Marzio 1, 50122 Florence, tel: (055) 287 216, fax: (055) 212 208, www.hermitagehotel.com.* Romantic and central – reach out and touch the Ponte Vecchio. Housed in a 13th-century tower and invitingly decorated with oriental runners and potted palms. A top-floor alfresco breakfast terrace offers sweeping views enjoyed by some of the newly refurbished rooms as well. 28 rooms.

Torre Guelfa €€ *Borgo Santissimi Apostoli 8, 50123 Florence, tel: (055) 239 6338, fax: (055) 239 8577, www.hoteltorreguelfa.com.* On an ultra-central cobbled side street, in an early Renaissance palazzo built around a medieval tower with breathtaking 360-degree views. Most room have canopied beds; all have new bathrooms. 12 rooms.

SANTA CROCE (EAST)

Locanda Orchidea € *Borgo degli Albizi 11, 50122 Florence, tel: (055) 248 0346, fax: (055) 248 0346, www.hotelorchideaflorence.it.* There are only a handful of rooms in this budget hotel, housed very close to the Duomo, in the 12th-century palazzo in which Dante's wife was born. Furniture is old and quirky, only one of the rooms has a shower (the others share newly refurbished communal bathrooms), but the place has bags of character and the windows are huge, making the rooms light and airy. One room has a pretty terrace. Closed for most of August. 7 rooms. No credit cards.

Plaza Hotel Lucchesi €€€€ *Lungarno della Zecca Vecchia 38, 50122 Florence, tel: (055) 26236, fax: (055) 248 0921, www.plaza lucchesi.it*. Elegant and friendly hotel overlooking the river (riverview and terraced rooms must be specially requested), a few blocks east of the Uffizi. 97 rooms.

SAN LORENZO AND SAN MARCO (NORTH)

Casci €–€€   *Via Cavour 13, 50129 Florence, tel: (055) 211 686, fax: (055) 239 6461, www.hotelcasci.com*. Simple, tastefully renovated rooms in a 15th-century building that was once the home of Gioacchino Rossini, the composer of *The Barber of Seville*. Run by an amiable family, and an easy stroll from the Duomo. 25 rooms.

Cimabue €€ *Via Benifacio Lupi 7, 50129 Florence, tel: (055) 475 601, fax: (055) 471 989, www.hotelcimabue.it*. Set in a quiet residential section just outside the centre, a charming setting with hospitable hosts. A leisurely half-hour stroll to the Duomo. 16 rooms.

Four Seasons Firenze €€€€ *Borgo Pinti 99, 50121 Florence, tel: (055) 26261, fax: (055) 262 6500, www.fourseasons.com/florence*. This newly opened, über-luxurious palazzo hotel is stunning, with frescoed ceilings, sumptuous furnishings and delightful gardens. None of this is cheap but staying here is certainly doing Florence in style. The excellent bar and restaurant are also worth checking out.

Il Guelfo Bianco €€€ *Via Cavour 29, 50129 Florence, tel: (055) 288 330, fax: (055) 295 203, www.ilguelfobianco.it*. An early 1990s newcomer in a 15th-century palazzo, furnished with some original antiques and with a friendly but correct staff, just north of the Duomo. 39 rooms.

Loggiato dei Serviti €€–€€€ *Piazza della SS Annunziata 3, 50122 Florence, tel: (055) 289 592, fax: (055) 289 595, www.loggiatodei servitihotel.it*. The name recalls the 16th-century Servite monastery once housed in this palazzo with loggia, set on a beautifully proportioned Renaissance piazza. Vaulted ceilings and imaginative design make each room unique. 29 rooms.

Mario's €€ *Via Faenza 89, 50123 Florence, tel: (055) 216 801, fax: (055) 212 039, www.hotelmarios.com.* Two blocks from the railway station, this decades-old favourite is impeccably maintained, owned and managed with warmth. Loyal clients keep coming back, and back again. 16 rooms.

Monna Lisa €€€€ *Borgo Pinti 27, 50121 Florence, tel: (055) 247 9751, fax: (055) 247 9755, www.hotelmonnalisaflorence.com.* In a landmark medieval palazzo, with original wooden ceilings, red-brick floors and lots of historical character. Rooms are generally small, the preferred (quieter) ones overlooking a central garden. Easy walk to both Duomo and Santa Croce. 30 rooms.

Regency €€€€ *Piazza M. d'Azeglio 3, 50121 Florence, tel: (055) 245 247, fax: (055) 234 6735, www.regency-hotel.com.* A refined 19th-century-style palazzo, attractively distinguished with antiques and a much-respected restaurant, situated on a leafy, quiet piazza in a residential corner of the city just east of the centre. Quite a walk for those not so accustomed. 34 rooms.

Residenza Johanna I € *Via Bonifacio Lupi 14, 50129 Florence, tel: (055) 481 896, fax: (055) 482 721, www.johanna.it.* One of a set of great-value-for-money residences across the city. Set in a residential area to the north of the centre, the rooms are comfortable and nicely decorated, but there are few hotel frills; not all rooms have attached baths. A do-it-yourself breakfast kit is provided in each room.

SANTA MARIA NOVELLA (WEST)

Astoria €€€€ *Via del Giglio 9, 50123 Florence, tel: (055) 239 8095, fax: (055) 214 632, http://astoria.boscolohotels.com.* Fine old Florentine palazzo, part of which dates from the 13th and 14th centuries, offering gracious rooms. Centrally located, equidistant to the Duomo and open-air market of San Lorenzo. 98 rooms.

Baglioni €€€€ *Piazza Unità Italiana 6, 50123 Florence, tel: (055) 23580, fax: (055) 235 8895, www.hotelbaglioni.it.* A dignified, well-run hotel just across the square from the railway station. A turn-of-the-20th-century bastion that boasts a roof-terrace restaurant offering fantastic views. 195 rooms.

Excelsior €€€€ *Piazza Ognissanti 3, 50123 Florence, tel: (055) 27151, fax: (055) 210 278, www.westin.com.* Old-fashioned elegance in Florence's grande-dame hotel, on the banks of the Arno. Recently refurbished with plush carpets, chaises longues, spacious bathrooms and grand public rooms. 168 rooms.

Grand €€€€ *Piazza Ognissanti 1, 50123 Florence, tel: (055) 27161, fax: (055) 217 400, www.westin.com.* Sister hotel to (and located across the piazza from) the Excelsior – both are run by the Starwood group. Similar level of luxury, but with a slightly more intimate and less commercialised ambience, some rooms with Renaissance-style frescoes. Recently refurbished. 107 rooms.

JK Place €€€€ *Piazza Santa Maria Novella 7, 50123 Florence, tel: (055) 264 5181, fax: (055) 265 8387, www.jkplace.com.* This chic and luxurious design hotel is tucked into the corner of Piazza Santa Maria Novella. The very elegant interiors contain works of art and classic designer furniture and lighting. The suites and penthouse are particularly impressive, and the terrace bar is also wonderful.

OLTRARNO (SOUTH)

Annalena €€€ *Via Romana 34, 50125 Florence, tel: (055) 222 402, fax: (055) 222 403, www.hotelannalena.it.* Tasteful hotel on first floor of a historically important palazzo from the 14th century; many rooms share a terrace overlooking a lovely private garden. Located across from the Pitti Palace and Boboli Garden. 20 rooms.

Lungarno €€€€ *Borgo S. Jacopo 14, 50125 Florence, tel: (055) 2726 4000, fax: (055) 268 437, www.lungarnohotels.com.* The only hotel directly on the (south) bank of the Arno, with half of its newly renovated rooms overlooking the Ponte Vecchio. Owned by the local scions of style and fashion, the Ferragamo family. Some rooms housed in an adjacent 15th-century tower. 73 rooms.

Recommended Restaurants

Central Florence is well supplied with cafés, bars, pizzerias, *trattorie* and restaurants. The further away from the tourist attractions you go, the less expensive they become. Many bars or cafés are beginning to offer light lunches as a *trattoria* alternative. Most restaurant bills will include a service charge *(servizio)* and a cover charge *(coperto)*, and in this case it is usual to leave a small tip of a few coins for the waiter. If service is not included, it is because they are used to a tourist clientele: tip using your judgement as you would normally, 10–15 percent being the norm.

Below is a list of recommended restaurants. Reservations are recommended for the more expensive establishments. Almost all restaurants close during the summer's hottest weeks, usually from the end of July to 1 September for one to three weeks. Cafés below offer three (light) meals; unless specified all others offer lunch and dinner only.

As a basic guide, we have used the following symbols to give an indication of the price of a three-course meal per person, including water and a bottle of house wine:

€€€€	over 65 euros
€€€	45–65 euros
€€	25–45 euros
€	below 25 euros

CENTRO STORICO (CENTRE)

Angels €€€ *Via del Proconsolo 29/31, tel: (055) 239 8762, www. ristoranteangels.it.* A chic bar and restaurant well known for its modern Italian cooking. Try dishes such as duck with balsamic vinegar and preserved fruits, or the gnocchi filled with pumpkin. The classy bar is open for cocktails and *aperitivi* from 6pm. Daily lunch and dinner.

Caffè Gilli €€ *Via Roma 1/r, tel: (055) 213 896, www.gilli.it.* Founded over 250 years ago, the Caffè Gilli is the plushest of all the cafés on the Piazza Repubblica. Redolent of a bygone era (particularly the old-fashioned interior), with its silver service and impeccable waiters. A traditional favourite place to rendezvous, it is famous for its chocolates and especially its *gianduja*. **Caffè Paszkowski** (next door, closed Monday) is known for its summer evenings with live music.

Caffè Rivoire €€ *Piazza della Signoria 5, tel: (055) 214 412, www. rivoire.it.* Arguably the most famous of all the history-steeped cafés for its ringside seat in Florence's most picturesque piazza, with Michelangelo's *David* before you. Outside seating is perfect for iced tea, light lunch and people-watching. Thick, dark hot chocolate is a local wintertime tradition. Activity flutters around the bar; proper service at the inside tables attracts society ladies of a certain age, along with foot-weary tourists. Closed Monday.

Cantinetta del Verrazzano € *Via dei Tavolini 18/20/r, tel: (055) 268 590.* Popular wine bar serving wines from the family vineyards in Chianti's Castello di Verrazzano. Great baked breads from the wood-burning ovens make this a great place to stop for a *merenda* (snack) or light meal, with a dozen Tuscan wines by the glass. Closed Sunday.

Coquinarius €€ *Via delle Oche 15r, tel: (055) 230 2153.* This tiny yet fashionable restaurant is always full, and you can eat here at almost any time of day. Try the lunch salads, the *carpaccio*, platters of cheese and cured meats or the rightfully famous pear and *pecorino ravioli*. Save some space for the exquisite homemade desserts. Morning to evening Monday to Saturday.

Gustavino €€€ *Via della Condotta 37r, tel: (055) 239 9806, www. gustavino.it.* This is a new and glossy restaurant whose open kitchen allows you to see your meal being prepared. The food is creative without being too elaborate or over-fussy, and is served beautifully on large white plates. Look out for the speciality wine-and-food evenings they run. The Canova wine bar next door is open daily (noon–late) for similar dishes but in a less formal atmosphere. Dinner only Monday to Friday, lunch and dinner Saturday and Sunday.

SANTA CROCE (EAST)

Acqua al Due €–€€ *Via di Vigna Vecchia 40/r, tel: (055) 284 170, www.acquaal2.it.* Restaurant behind the Bargello known for its pasta: the signature dish is the pasta sampler plate with five varieties (with an occasional *risotto* thrown in). Second courses are available, but usually skipped for the dessert sampler. Locals, tourists, students and families share communal tables. Daily dinner.

Baldovino Enoteca €€ *Via San Giuseppe 18r, tel: (055) 234 7220, www.baldovino.com*. Run by Scotsman David Gardner, this modern, intimate wine bar-cum-restaurant serves up an interesting mix of well-cooked dishes culled from different cuisines. Its *trattoria* close by serves traditional Tuscan food. Daily lunch and dinner.

Il Cibreo Trattoria €€ *Via dei Macci 118/r, tel: (055) 234 1100*. Simple, *trattoria*-style restaurant that adopts a modern approach to classic Florentine dishes (i.e. no pasta) – *pappa al pomodoro* (a thick garlic-flavoured soup of bread and tomato), *piccione farcito con mostarda di frutta* (pigeon stuffed with spiced fruit), *palombo giovane alla livornese* (Livorno-style dove). Excellent desserts. The adjacent restaurant is widely acclaimed. It shares the same kitchen, but is far more expensive and formal and requires reservations, often far in advance. Closed Sunday and Monday.

Enoteca Pinchiori €€€€ *Via Ghibellina 87, tel: (055) 242 777, www.enotecapinchiorri.com*. One of the best and most famous restaurants in Italy, with one of the world's greatest wine cellars. The menu blends French and Tuscan influences. Think sparkling chandeliers, silver cloches and impeccable service. Formal dress. Closed Sunday and Monday and lunchtime on Tuesday and Wednesday.

Icche C'è C'è €€ *Via dei Magalotti 11/r, tel: (055) 216 589*. A rough translation of the name might be 'We've got what we've got' – in other words, ask what today's special is. It's an enjoyable and friendly establishment that serves good Florentine fare such as *ribollita* and *stracotto*. Closed Monday.

Osteria del Caffè Italiano €–€€€ *Via Isola delle Stinche 11/13, tel: (055) 289 368, www.caffeitaliano.it*. An imposing early Renaissance palazzo houses the Caffè Italiano pizzeria and *osteria*. The former offers just three types of pizza, all delicious. The latter serves good wines with carefully matched *salumi* (country-style salami and cheese) at lunchtime, and classic seasonal dishes in the evening. Closed Monday.

Il Pizzaiuolo € *Via dei Macci 113/r, tel: (055) 241 171.* Reservations are necessarry at this hopping pizzeria which offers just two seatings – at 7.30pm and at 9pm. A Neopolitan *pizzaiuolo* reigns over the wood-burning oven, turning out thick chewy-crusted pizza. There is a *trattoria* menu offering traditional Tuscan fare, but pizza is a must – at least as a table-shared appetiser to start the evening off. No credit cards. Closed Sunday.

SAN LORENZO AND SAN MARCO (NORTH)

Nerbone € *Piazza del Mercato Centrale, inside the market, tel: (055) 219 949.* One of the most popular lunch spots of the area, Nerbone serves up local dishes featuring seasonal ingredients and a daily menu. The *bollito* sandwich, with boiled meat, is a favourite. Lunch only Monday to Saturday.

La Pentola dell'Oro €€–€€€ *Via di Mezzo 24/26r, tel: (055) 241 808, www.lapentoladelloro.it.* As well as being unique, this is one of the friendliest restaurants in the city. Chef Giuseppe Alessi is more than willing to explain the dishes; the recipes are inspired by Medieval and Renaissance cookery. Dinner only Monday to Saturday, September to July.

Zà-Zà €€ *Piazza Mercato Centrale 26, tel: (055) 215 411, www.trattoriazaza.it.* Traditional Tuscan fare served at communal wooden tables frequented by tourists and market vendors and shoppers alike. Try the *crostini misti*, *ribollita* or the famous *bistecca*. Closed Sunday.

SANTA MARIA NOVELLA (WEST)

Buca Lapi €€€ *Via del Trebbio 1r, tel: (055) 213 768, www.buca lapi.com.* In the cellar of the Palazzo Antinori, this charming restaurant is regarded as serving one of the best *bistecca alla fiorentina* (enormous and beautifully grilled). As expected, being in the basement of the palazzo of one of Tuscany's best wine producers, it has an excellent range of wines. Dinner only Monday to Saturday.

Coco Lezzone €€ *Via del Parioncino 26/r, tel: (055) 287 178, fax: (055) 280 349.* A small, popular, no-frills institution off the elite shopping strip Via Tornabuoni, serving classic Florentine food on small tables with red-and-white checked cloths. Try the tasty pasta with porcini mushrooms. Closed Sunday and Tuesday evening. No credit cards.

Sostanza €€ *Via della Porcellana 25/r, tel: (055) 212 691.* Established in 1869, this casual *trattoria* near Piazza Santa Maria Novella offers minestrone, tripe, fried chicken and *stracotto*, but most come for the acclaimed Ferragamo *fiorentina* (after all, this place originated as a butcher's shop). Don't miss the *frittata di carciofi* (artichoke omelette) in season. No credit cards. Closed Saturday and Sunday.

OLTRARNO (SOUTH)

Antica Mescita € *Via di San Niccolò 60r, tel: (055) 234 2836.* This *osteria* in Oltrarno does simple and cheap, but extremely good, Italian food served up in a cheery, crowded atmosphere. Part of the eatery is set in a former chapel. Closed Sunday.

Bevo Vino € *Via di San Niccolò 59r, tel: (055) 200 1709.* A lovely medium-sized *enoteca*, offering daily first and second courses, *carpaccio* and *bruschetta*. It has good wine and cheese selections and the service is friendly and knowledgeable. During the summer outdoor seating is available. Daily noon until late.

Borgo Antico €–€€ *Piazza Santo Spirito 6/r, tel: (055) 210 437, www.borgoanticofirenze.com. Reservations not accepted: first come, first served.* Jam-packed pizzeria known for great thin-crusted pizzas in a lively atmosphere. Young, often abrupt staff. There is a full menu as well, but grab a coveted outdoor piazza table and stick with a simple pizza, salad and carafe of house wine. Daily.

Cavolo Nero €€€ *Via dell'Ardiglione 22, tel: (055) 294 744, www. cavolonero.it*. Not far from Piazza del Carmine (turn right off Via Santa Monaca) is the 'black cabbage' (named after a vital ingredient in *ribollita*). It is an elegant-looking well-lit place specialising in Mediterranean food such as couscous salad, *gazpacho*, grilled octopus and some great handmade pasta. It is not on the main tourist trail, though it is becoming more well known. Dinner only Monday to Saturday.

Filipepe €€€ *Via di San Niccolò 39r, tel: (055) 200 1397, www. filipepe.com*. Filipepe is an elegant take on modern Mediterranean cuisine. Soft candle lighting, cove ceilings, and the bottles of wine lining the walls give each area a private, yet comfortable feel. Filipepe's menu offers a seasonal selection of typical ingredients, frequently from the southern regions of Italy, including different kinds of *carpaccio*, salads, soups and pastas. There is a small outdoor area for the summer. Daily noon to late.

Osteria del Cinghiale Bianco €€ *Borgo S. Jacopo 43/r, tel: (055) 215 706, www.cinghialebianco.it*. Traditional dishes including hard-to-find *cinghiale* (wild boar) are even tastier in the medieval, mood-setting ambience accented by a few romantic niche tables. If *cinghiale* is not for you, there's a wide selection of simple classic Tuscan fare. Great choice for Sunday or Monday when most other restaurants are closed. Closed Tuesday and Wednesday.

Pitti Gola e Cantina € *Piazza de' Pitti 16, tel: (055) 212 704*. Lined with shelving containing innumerable bottles of wine, many available by the glass, this is a great little *enoteca*. Simple but tasty plates of *salumi* and cheese help the wine slip down. Daily morning to evening.

Le Volpi e l'Uva € *Piazza dei Rossi 1, tel: (055) 239 8132, www. levolpieluva.com*. This superb little wine bar has, surprise, a fantastic selection of Italian wines, including quite a number of little-known vintages from small producers. It also serves very tasty plates of cheese and *salumi*, as well as *schiacciatine* (thin flat bread) and hot focaccia topped with mushrooms and prosciutto. Monday to Saturday noon to evening.

INDEX

Berlitz pocket guide

Florence

Thirteenth Edition 2009

Written by Patricia Schultz
Updated by Maria Lord
Edited by Anna Tyler
Series Editor: Tony Halliday

Photography credits
Chris Coe 37; Jerry Dennis 6, 14, 17, 18, 28, 39, 40, 53, 63, 65; Guglielmo Galvin & George Taylor 79, 81; Frances Gransden 48, 57, 62, 73; Hans Höfer 21; istockphoto 1, 60; Britta Jaschinski 10, 11, 12, 13, 24, 26, 31, 32, 36, 43, 50, 52, 58, 59, 64, 67, 70, 71, 75, 76, 84, 86, 87, 88, 89, 90, 92, 97, 98, 99, 100, 101, 102; Anna Mockford & Nick Bonetti 8, 33, 35, 45, 47, 55, 68, 83, 94; Topfoto 23.

Cover picture: 4Corners Images

All Rights Reserved
© 2009 Berlitz Publishing/Apa Publications GmbH & Co. Verlag KG, Singapore Branch, Singapore

Printed in Singapore by Insight Print Services (Pte) Ltd, 38 Joo Koon Road, Singapore 628990. Tel: (65) 6865-1600. Fax: (65) 6861-6438

Berlitz Trademark Reg. U.S. Patent Office and other countries. Marca Registrada

Every effort has been made to provide accurate information in this publication, but changes are inevitable. The publisher cannot be responsible for any resulting loss, inconvenience or injury.

Contact us

At Berlitz we strive to keep our guides as accurate and up to date as possible, but if you find anything that has changed, or if you have any suggestions on ways to improve this guide, then we would be delighted to hear from you.

Berlitz Publishing, PO Box 7910, London SE1 1WE, England.
fax: (44) 20 7403 0290
email: berlitz@apaguide.co.uk
www.berlitzpublishing.com